# READING THE TAROT

## Workbook of Mastering the Mystery

Dawn Grey

# READING THE TAROT

By Dawn Grey, Certified Tarot Master Instructor

©2010 Dawn Grey

**Reading the Tarot**

1st Edition

Copyright ©2010 by Dawn Grey

ISBN-13:
978-1456489991

ISBN-10:
1456489992

Rights Owner: Dawn Grey

Printed in the United States of America

All Rights Reserved. No part of this book may be reproduced in any form, except brief excerpts for the purpose of review, without written permission of the publisher.

All artwork © 1909 Rider-Waite-Smith Tarot Deck, public domain archives

To contact the author, you may email Dawn Grey at
reikirays@yahoo.com

**Please visit our web sites**

**World Metaphysical Association www.worldmeta.org
Reiki Rays Institute www.reikiraysinstitute.com**

Welcome. You are ready to begin what can be the most exciting journey you have ever partaken: the Journey of the Tarot. The purpose of this book is to help you discover how to be the best Tarot reader you can be by understanding the history, archetypes, and symbols of the Tarot throughout the ages.

While taking your Tarot journey, do not be surprised, however, if you reap deeper rewards. Learning the Tarot will reveal to you insight into your character and core being, thus propelling you further on your spiritual path.

READING THE TAROT was written to be a useful tool for the novice and expert alike. New seekers will encounter all the practical information, history, and substance of Tarot in a fun, easy-to-read guide. Intermediates will have the opportunity to advance their skills with numerous exercises that allow the reader to connect book knowledge with personal exploration. The advanced practitioner will discover new insight and discussion on Tarot not readily available in books.

This manual is the result of seventeen years of reading and teaching the tarot. I offer this book as a stand alone guide to the general public, and as a supplement to the official Tarot course of The World Metaphysical Association Academy.

As such, READING THE TAROT is suitable as a "teach yourself" guide, a group study workbook, or a formal manual for workshops and courses. Whichever path you take, you will find INSIGHT TAROT will be helpful every step of the way.

Enjoy!

**Dawn Grey**

# Acknowledgements

I wish to thank the following individuals for their contribution to this book:

Reverend Dr. John Gilbert, founder of The Tarot Institute, for your many years of teaching, motivation, and encouragement throughout my Tarot journey. I am forever grateful for your assistance and friendship.

Frank Atwood for his tireless editorial efforts, patience, and dedication.

Mari Geasair for her inspiration.

Gary Shainheit for his technical and literary assistance.

My husband, Mark, for his continued support and comfort.

Swami Jyoti Chakrananda, for her humble advice and teachings.

To all my students past and present for your numerous requests for a full-length instruction manual.

Most of all, to you, the reader, for your interest in carrying on the Tarot tradition. May these pages bring to you much knowledge and insight.

# Table of Contents

**Lesson One -** Getting Started with Tarot — page 11

**Lesson Two -** The Minor Arcana & Simple Card Interpretation — page 33

**Lesson Three -** The Suit of Swords — page 45

**Lesson Four -** The Suits of Wands and Cups — page 55

**Lesson Five -** The Suit of Pentacles — page 67

**Lesson Six -** The Numbers and Suit Meanings — page 75

**Lesson Seven** Court Cards — page 89

**Lesson Eight -** Reversed Cards — page 111

**Lesson Nine -** Overview of the Major Arcana — page 122

**Lesson Ten -** Major Arcana 0 to 7 — page 146

**Lesson Eleven -** Major Arcana 8 to 14 — page 155

**Lesson Twelve -** Major Arcana 15 to 21 — page 163

**Lesson Thirteen** – Mastering the Art of Tarot Reading — page 171

**Lesson Fourteen -** Working with Spreads — page 184

**Lesson Fifteen -** Reading for Yourself and Others — page 199

# Lesson One
# Getting Started with Tarot

- What Exactly Is Tarot?
- Why Study Tarot?
- Choosing a Deck and Gathering Your Tools
- Preparing Mentally to Do Intuitive Work
- Grounding and Setting "Working Space"
- Working with Your First Card
- Completing Your Work

## What Exactly Is the Tarot?

The Tarot is an ancient method of teaching universal and spiritual concepts, which in turn assists the seeker in gaining insight into one's character, present circumstances, and future possibilities. The word Tarot refers to the physical deck of 78 cards with archetypal and symbolic pictures as well as the art of learning and interpreting the traditions associated with these cards.

The Tarot's history is undocumented prior to the 1400's, when the earliest existing cards were discovered. This special deck was painted to honor a marriage between the Visconti and the Sforza families, two well established noble Italian households at that time. The Visconti-Sforza Tarot is still in print and very popular even today.

It is assumed that the Tarot was kept secret to protect both its wisdom as well as its teachers. The average person was not literate, so the fact that the Tarot relied on pictures to teach spiritual exploration to the masses was likely seen as a threat to the priests and leaders of the time.

The Tarot, nonetheless, became extremely popular and was widely used. In the past, most people first encountered the Tarot as a gambling game called Tarochi, but others approached the cards for fortunetelling as well as for spiritual exploration. As time passed, the game element of Tarot has diminished but there has been much exploration of the Tarot's meanings. Modern thinkers such as Carl Jung and Walt Whitman have delved deeply into the mysteries of Tarot, and the popularity of this ancient tool skyrocketed in modern times. During the early 1960's there were only two Tarot decks that were widely distributed to bookstores. At present, there are over 1200 available decks, with themes from Baseball to Hello Kitty and just about everything in between. Tarot is certainly in high demand.

A traditional Tarot deck consists of 78 cards. The first 22 cards are called the Major Arcana which depicts the Universal Journey of the Soul, and the remaining 56 cards are called the Minor Arcana which depict the day to day events of life. The Minor Arcana is separated into four groups, each represented by a suit focusing on one of the four elements, swords for air, wands for fire, cups for water, and pentacles for earth.

One of the most misunderstood points of Tarot is how it is interpreted. Many people focus solely on learning individual cards, especially the Major Arcana, and dismiss the rest of the deck. In fact, there are decks currently in print that only offer the Major Arcana. However, the real understanding of the Tarot comes from understanding it as a unit and learning how the cards relate to one another. The Tarot is a story that unfolds in sequential order, with key symbols and themes following throughout. While you certainly can choose to learn or meditate on the symbols one card at a time, to truly master the Tarot you will need a working knowledge of all the cards of the deck, as every card has equal importance. It is a fallacy to think that the Major Arcana have significance over the Minor Arcana, or that Aces are inferior to Kings.

While there is much intellectual study of the Tarot available, it was created to be a symbolic study of images. Therefore, while memorizing the symbols and their meanings has its relevance, its true mysteries lie in what insight those symbols hold for the individual reader.

Like any spiritual tool or work of art, interpretation will grow and change over time as the experience and understanding of the observer deepens. It is possible to see things in a card, even after years of intense study, that you have never seen before. For this reason, it is presumptuous to state that any single card has one set meaning. Although many who have worked with the cards for a while will state that "the cards never lie" the meaning of the Wheel of Fortune may affect you slightly differently today than it did yesterday, and who knows for sure how it will greet you tomorrow.

# Why Study Tarot?

I am often asked this question by new students and skeptics alike and regardless of how many times I am asked, the answer is always the same. While there are countless esoteric and spiritual answers, the two most practical reasons that relate to all individuals of all backgrounds is that studying the Tarot will make you more intuitive and improve your ability to relate with others. I know this to be true from my own personal experience, as well as from the feedback of hundreds of students, clients, and gatherings I have hosted over the years.

## Stronger Intuition

Most Tarot practitioners, from beginners to teachers to masters, agree that intuitive talent is something that everyone is born with to some degree. It is also agreed upon by most that Tarot will increase and fine-tune this natural ability. However, this does not mean that the simple act of owning a deck, enrolling in a course, or reading (or writing) a book will dramatically improve your innate skills automatically. You may not be able to play the piano or sing in public, but most people can tap out a simple rhythm or learn to sing along with Happy Birthday. In fact, although most people will tell you they have no musical ability at all, less than 1% of the world population is actually musically impaired (unable to either distinguish between tones or follow simple rhythm.) The same holds true for the average person learning the basics of intuitive perception.

Tarot is a tool for teaching the building blocks of intuition in a fun and engaging way. It shows people the natural patterns in psychic perception and phenomenon, in a simple game-like way. By repeated exposure to Tarot images and ideas, we learn how to follow and manipulate intuitive and psychic energy patterns on our own without even realizing it is happening. This is why a great amount of Tarot readers discover after a few years that they have also become quite adept at other psychic arts without really trying. In time, Tarot readers become proficient in the language of the Tarot, the language of archetype and symbolism, and discover how to balance ancient teachings with personal intuition.

## Better Relationships

The second part of my answer, "studying Tarot will improve your relationships," grows out of learning the language and archetypes of Tarot. But how exactly can understanding symbols build better relationships? Simple. There are three core ingredients that everyone needs to have great relationships. Most of us have one or maybe two components, but it is the rare person that comes up with all three without hard work and careful study.

**These ingredients are:**

1) A Good Relationship with Yourself

2) Social Skills

3) Appropriate Timing

If we can learn to make each of these three ingredients work for us, we can discover the joy and ease of relationships instead of focusing on the work and confusion of relationships that don't incorporate all these factors. These factors are just as true for romantic as well as platonic relationships.

## A Process for Developing Self-Love

We have all heard that we need to love ourselves before we can expect anyone else to love us. This one is a favorite truism of anyone dispensing advice, from professional psychotherapists and talk show hosts to late night advertisements for self-help books. It is good advice as far as it goes, but the problem is that it is rarely explained how to develop this all-important but often elusive sense of self-love. Let me demystify the process for you.

Self-love comes from the age-old desire to "Know Thy Self". Tarot can provide us with a fresh set of tools to do just that. Every time we explore a card or a specific symbol, we are in truth exploring ourselves. In addition, working with the deck gives us a fresh look at how to accomplish self-acceptance and enjoy our personal relationship with our self.

One of the most beautiful components of the Tarot is what is called The Fool's Journey, which depicts the important life lessons we all encounter, and offers us valuable information for making the journey of these lessons both fun and rewarding. It also helps reveal to us how we can master challenging life lessons as they come up. Knowing the map of The Fool connects us to deeper spiritual meanings and to understand that everybody, from housewife to scholar, ultimately walks the same journey. We are all on a spiritual journey. The only difference is where we are on the path at this present moment and where we choose to go from here.

## A Tool for Developing Social Skills

There are some people for whom communication and relationships come natural, whereas most would say that people skills are not as easy or natural as it appears. All of us have encountered some people with whom we instantly resonate with, and others that no matter how hard we try we just can't.

The reasons for this are embodied in the Tarot. The Minor Arcana, and particularly the Court Cards, have hidden in their symbolism important clues to learning our own relationship techniques; through understanding what type of person we are and how we best interact with other types of people. The information is there, we simply need to learn to unlock it.

## Tarot and Free Will

There has been much controversy about whether or not Tarot violates free will by revealing future events. This so-called predictive ability has become THE advertising ploy by many 900 lines and fortunetellers, but it simply is not the true manner in which the Tarot works. The Tarot is not a fortunetelling device in the way they have been presented but a symbolic tool for self-discovery. However, these archetypal images do reveal to us our patterns and obstacles, so when Tarot "predicts" it does so by showing us if we do not change our behavior we are likely to be in the same situations again and again.

Therefore, the Tarot shows us what road we are on. Just because our behavior has been revealed to us does not mean it takes away our free will. What the Tarot does is give us the insight, and the choice of whether or not to take that insight into consideration. The cards are there to point out the issues, but we are ultimately responsible for discovering the solutions. Those fortunetellers who work with fear and control see these patterns, and rather than inform their client, use that information against them to try to persuade them to purchase more readings, additional services, remove hexes, or other such ploys for additional cash. So, it is not the Tarot itself but the ethics of the reader that can compromise free will. Don't fall for false promises and flashing neon lights.

## Help with the All-Important Question of Timing

Timing is perhaps the most overlooked relationship skill of all. Expressing appreciation, asking for a favor, sharing a concern, or even going out and having some fun can backfire if the timing is wrong. Too often when this happens we either blame the relationship or blame ourselves. We decide that Jane turned us down for that important favor because she does not value the friendship, or that we had a lousy time on the date because we were with the wrong person (or that we are somehow undesirable). These ideas are certainly possibilities, but they are not the only possibilities. Often the case is that we simply exercised poor timing. Jane was preoccupied with work problems, or our outing was scheduled during a time of family conflict. This is where the Tarot can be of assistance. As a mirror of the self, it can reveal to us optimum timing for such events, or help us see that we are preoccupied or not ready to give our full attention to an event or issue. So if used correctly, the Tarot is a tool for transforming your relationship with yourself and the world by reclaiming your intuitive and practical power.

## Choosing a Deck

Now that you understand a bit about what Tarot is and what its study can bring to you, you will need to get a Tarot Deck. Unlike many Tarot courses this class is designed to work with almost any 78card deck because it teaches the structure and deeper meanings of the cards, rather than discussing the cards one by one and symbol by symbol. If you have already worked with Tarot and have a deck you like, please use that deck. If you are new to Tarot and do not have a deck, here are some suggestions on choosing your deck:

- Make sure it is really a Tarot deck. There are many other divination decks on the market, as well as decks with the name Tarot by a publisher who does not know what Tarot really is. Oracle decks such as those depicting angels, key words, or motivational phrases are wonderful tools, but are not Tarot decks and will not be suitable for this program. However, it is not complicated to Tarot deck that you will like and will work for you. As mentioned earlier, a true Tarot deck almost always has 78 cards, so counting the cards is your first clue. Beyond that there should be obvious groupings of the cards into "suit" cards and a series of 22 other cards usually referred to as Major Arcana or Greater Secrets or some other special title. (I am not being vague here on purpose as there are literally hundreds of decks with varying titles for the Major Arcana and suits). When in doubt ask the shopkeeper or your instructor whether the deck you are considering is truly a traditional Tarot deck. While many of the themed decks might be fun to collect, you may have difficulty using the deck if the chosen theme is foreign to you.

- Make sure it has full pictures on all the cards. Some older, more "occult" decks will have pictures of people or events on the Major Arcana cards but not the Minor Arcana. They will instead simply have the number and then a geometrical drawing showing that many of that suit's symbol. These decks might be fine once you have mastered the Tarot, but to learn how to use the Tarot you need full understanding of their symbols, so blank or otherwise incomplete cards will not work for this stage of your learning. If the shop does not have a sample card to view, go online and do your research. Then you can purchase or special order your deck with the merchant of your choice.

- Make sure you like it. You will be looking at your deck a lot. If you find the pictures too disturbing, depicting too much nudity, or so vague that you really can't decipher the meaning from the image, move on to another. Get one that speaks to you and that you find inspiring and interesting to look at. Just because one person swears by the Hanson-Roberts deck or your favorite reader uses the Osho Zen does not mean this will provide you the same level of accuracy. Use your insight and get what works, and discard what doesn't.

You may have heard that you must have your Tarot deck given to you for it to work, and this is far from the truth. This tradition stems from when learning Tarot was an apprenticed skill, and your deck was hand made and given to you by your teacher. It is absolutely fine to get one for yourself and is actually encouraged.

You will also want a special bag or container to keep your cards so that they stay clean and feel special. I personally have a box with an assortment of crystals and gemstones in it, which I believe enhance my intuition and help absorb the energies of the clients. Many books discuss wrapping the cards in silk or another natural fabric. All of these suggestions will work if you are in agreement with them. If toting your cards around in a brown paper bag calls to you, then do it. If you want to invest in an elaborate jewelry box or container, that's fine too. Just honor your insight.

In addition to your deck you will also need a notebook where you can record your class exercises and where you can also write down notes about your own spiritual thoughts and readings. This we will refer to in class as your Tarot journal. While this text offers several exercises with blank spaces to write your answers, some exercises are just too personal or far too in-depth to fit in the spaces provided. Plus, you are likely to do some exercises over and over again, so having a formal journal is very helpful. Also, it's a great learning tool to record your readings, then in the future see if they were truly accurate.

## Shuffling Your Deck

Many new readers ask about the right way to shuffle. Since we are working with Reversed cards in this course, you will need to truly scatter the cards up and down, taking some out of the deck and putting them back in so that you know there will be the possibility of reversed cards. You should shuffle in any way that is convenient for you, but it needs to be consistent. If for instance your shuffling routine is to shuffle them for a set number of times, tell that to your deck to set your intention. If you choose to shuffle, then cut the cards, tell your deck that from now on this deck will be used in this way. It really doesn't matter so long as it stays the same.

Just as there is a lot of talk about whether or not you should buy your own deck, there is a lot of discussion as to whether or not you should let others touch or shuffle your cards. I know that for me, when I am giving a reading to a client I simply must have their energy on the cards, otherwise I get a reading suited more for myself than them. I found that the energy of the last person that touched them is the energy that attracts the reading.

Keeping this in mind, you need to thoroughly shuffle cards in between readings so that the previous client's energy is removed. My trick for this is to knock on the cards three or more times, then shuffle the cards until the deck does not want to smoothly go back together. I call this when the cards "fight with me". I see this as my signal to turn the cards over to my client. If I am doing a reading for myself, I cut the deck, and proceed to lay them out into the spread of my choice.

If having another person touching your cards simply doesn't feel right to you, I advise having a separate deck for your personal readings and another for professional use. It can be the same exact deck or another deck.

When it comes to flipping the cards over once placed in a spread, be very careful to flip them from side to side and not up to down. Since in this course we will be working with Reversed cards, you cannot flip the cards from up to down, as this will interfere with their position, making upright cards into reversed, and vice versa.

## Preparing to Do Intuitive Work

The first step in working intuitively with the Tarot, whether you are a beginner or an old pro is to mentally prepare. You will want to do this every time you work with the cards from now on. Be sure to take time to do the exercise in this section several times until you feel completely comfortable with it.

The most important element to opening up and learning how to use your own psychic abilities, which is a major requirement for learning Tarot, is the sincere and deep-felt belief that you have psychic talents. Skepticism is valuable when exploring the hows and whys of those abilities, but it is a major stumbling block to really getting them in gear. If you can understand that the Universe is, first and foremost, energy, and that you are not just connected to the energy but are a part of it, it makes it much easier to trust your abilities that come from this Source.

# Exercise 1A: Sensing Energy

Sit quietly and let yourself feel the energy flowing through your body. You may think of this energy as light or heat or simply sensations. However, you experience it is fine. If you have to imagine feeling it, that's fine. After a while the imagination shifts and becomes real. After you are comfortable with the flow, feel it coming in through the top of your head and going out at the soles of your feet. If you wish you can imagine that on the way through your body this energy picks up and takes with it any counterproductive energy you may be holding in your body such as tiredness or destructive emotions or just mental "junk". Note: this exercise is also helpful for quieting anxiety and stress. Record your experience in the spaces provided or in your journal.

# Exercise 1B: Setting Your "Working Space"

Once you have begun to feel what it is like to "turn on your intuitive radio" you are ready to begin your Tarot study in earnest. The first step to working with the Tarot is always to ground and set a working space, also referred to as a "sacred space" in many traditions.

Setting your sacred space is a simple concept. Essentially it is the process of allowing your unconscious mind to understand that "now" is the time to be intuitively and spiritually open. Despite the perceived glamour of suddenly getting intuitive impressions, there are times when you just do not want to get insight into the people and situations around you. Grocery shopping, riding the bus, standing in line, and a host of other daily activities are much easier if you are not psychically "tuned in" to those around you. Furthermore, it is rude and inappropriate to be receiving intuitive insight about others without first obtaining specific permission. For this reason, it is imperative that before you start working to open up your intuitive abilities you give your inner-self a clear sense of the rules. Essentially, telling it when and when not to open up to intuitive and spiritual impressions is one of the best guidelines to follow in the beginning. As your gift matures you can modify this process to enhance your psychic skills.

For now, simply set your "now" or "on" signal by setting aside the time and space in which you work on learning Tarot as special and ideally set aside only for this work. If you do not have a space that you can dedicate only to Tarot and spiritual study that is fine. You can be creative by gathering a nice tablecloth that is only set out for readings for instance. Either way, the first step is to make sure that you are physically comfortable and relatively free of interruptions. This might be tempting but don't do it. It will set you up for psychic complications you don't want down the road. There is a reason the old style card readers made such a big production of the silk scarf on the head, the special carved box, and the incense. It sets up a ceremony and creates the transition from mundane into spiritual. It also signals to friends and family that consulting the cards is a sacred act and not a game to be played on a whim.

1) Make sure that you are in an area where you are uninterrupted and either alone or with people who support what you are doing. Make sure it is "your" space. Turn off the phone, shoo away the kids and roommates, etc., and make sure that they will not burst in on your session.

2) Make sure you are physically comfortable and the space is clean, and contains no distractions such as a pile of bills or "to do" things in sight. These distractions could pull you mentally off track and diminish the clarity of your reading, as well as distract your client. I will never forget when I did readings in a room that doubled as an art gallery and one artist's work was so unusual to clients that their focus was more on trying to figure out her art than their own readings.

3) Make sure you are ready and in the right frame on mind to do a reading. Poor health can interfere with your focus, but so can a client who is not taking the Tarot seriously, has unrealistic demands, etc.

4) It is very helpful to have a specific physical signal for your Higher Self to take as the "start" cue. Your cue can be something "traditional" like laying a special cloth out, lighting a candle, or it can be something entirely personal like placing objects of personal power near you. Your special cue will be very helpful later on when you are having a bad day and it is not as easy as normal to tune in. By repeating your signal, you automatically shift your brain waves to a similar state as last time you used the signal- remember Pavlov? For this reason, do not abuse your signal. Pick something unique and use it only when you do Tarot. Record your choice(s) below.

_____
_____
_____
_____
_____

5) The next step to setting your space is to formally acknowledge your intent. This helps keep you from getting any conflicting or disturbing psychic energy that you do not need. Say it, write it, or think it strongly. It really does not matter how you do it, simply that you do it. Setting intent is a powerful technique and it works, but the power is in the fact that you set a clear intent, not in how you set it. Intention is the same power behind prayer, ceremonies, even Feng Shui, and practitioners of all of these will insist that it is not actually the system but the intent in harnessing the energy that creates the desired outcome. If you do not have any idea about intent, or do not know how to form a psychic intent do not worry. We will talk more about this later in the book, but for now you can simply state something like the following: "May this reading be for the good of all, respect the free will of all, and provide exactly what is needed to assist this client at this time. Any energies or intents that are not in agreement with this intent are not welcome here." What is your intention, and how will you reinforce it in your space? Record your answers here.

_____
_____
_____
_____
_____
_____
_____
_____
_____
_____
_____
_____
_____
_____

# Exercise 1C: Grounding

Grounding is a process of casting aside your personal "mental clutter" so that you will have an easier time recognizing and properly interpreting information that comes to you through psychic means. This is one of the most important steps in any type of psychic work, and doing it properly can help you to avoid many pitfalls and mistakes that are common for Tarot readers. We will be discussing it in depth throughout the class, so for now just take some time to get comfortable with this simple grounding exercise. Don't forget to do this or another grounding technique you have learned elsewhere before and after each Tarot session.

1) Confirm that you have set up your working space and that you will be reasonably undisturbed.

2) Confirm and re-state your intention for the work that you are doing.

3) Do the energy feeling exercise described above in the "mentally preparing for psychic work" section.

4) Take a few deep breaths and when you exhale imagine any and all unwanted energy, thoughts, emotions, physical stress, or distraction flowing into the earth. As you breathe allow yourself to fill with fresh clean energy and to release any and all distracting energy. If you are new to this type of thing it might help you to visualize the energy as light moving through your body, or to imagine feeling it as a light humming vibration working its way through your body. It does not matter if you "feel" it. If you imagine it with sincerity this energetic shift will come with time and practice.

5) Very clearly imagine, or tell yourself mentally, or both, that you have an energetic "root" that channels energy from you to the earth. All energies, pieces of information, and insights that come to you through your work with the Tarot will move through this channel. You can reach into it and obtain any information or energy you need, but you do not have to directly experience this energy if you do not choose to do so. This helps you to stay fresh and not burn out your personal energy to do

readings. If you are reading for others, or doing a particularly long and in-depth reading for your self, this can be especially helpful. Once you have imagined this, simply tell yourself that the process will continue throughout your entire session. Write down your experience and how you felt during each step of the process.

_____
_____
_____
_____
_____
_____
_____
_____
_____

## Exercise 1D: Working with Your First Card

A final step in your introduction to working with the Tarot is to learn how to deeply observe the symbols on each card. In later lessons, we will delve more into traditional associations for the cards, but they will be most meaningful to you if you have already learned to explore and understand the cards for yourself. The Tarot is by definition an art form that draws on universal symbols and archetypes that we can all relate to on some personal and spiritual level. Giving yourself the gift of deeply exploring the artwork will open up your intuition and imagination, even if you never look at another deck again. Please note that this will be harder for those with experience than those who are more a beginner. If you are an experienced reader, challenge yourself to look at each card with fresh eyes and allow yourself to find visual proof of the information that you believe you "know". You may benefit more if you use a different, newer deck should you find this is your situation.

All you need to do is shuffle your deck, choose a card, study it intently, and create a meaning. You can create a meaning for the card in general, or you can tailor it to a concern or question you are currently struggling with in your own life. The key however is to really look at every single detail, color, symbol, action, and the card number or title. Often people make the mistake of thinking more about what a card "should" mean than allowing the card to shown them what it really does mean for them.

Most people approach the Tarot by trying to learn and memorize set meanings for each of the cards. While there may be some validity to establishing keywords or phrases, most readers try to pick their meaning way too soon before getting to really know the cards first. This also holds true of those who have received many card readings and are assuming the interpretations of their reader. As a result, they never really see their cards except through the lenses of preconception.

The best thing you can do to get the most out of your Tarot experience is to get used to looking for the symbolic clues right from the beginning. Also remember that no matter what meaning you find for a card someone at some time created that meaning from their own experience and observation. The person who came up with the meaning became the "expert" by studying the card and then sharing that meaning with others. Allow yourself to be your own expert and study the cards just as carefully.

1) Perform your grounding procedure. Next, spend time in your reading space studying your deck or web page of Tarot Cards. Examine each card thoroughly.

2) Choose a card at random to carefully study. Write down everything you notice: including the color, the details, what is in the background, and any symbols whether you understand them or not.

_____
_____
_____
_____
_____
_____
_____
_____
_____
_____
_____
_____
_____
_____
_____
_____
_____
_____
_____
_____
_____

3) Now create a meaning. Do not look one up or try to remember what you might have already been told it means. After studying the features in the card, what makes a logical definition for the card? Just make it up like you were using it to tell a story to a child. **HINT:** If you cannot come up with anything you probably skipped steps or worked through them too fast.

_____
_____
_____
_____

4) Finally, but only if you want, you can now compare your meaning to what others define the card as. If you do not have access to Tarot books this can be found on the Internet. Remember the point of this final step is not to decide if you were right or wrong, but rather just to see how well you were able on first attempt to open up your intuition and allow the card to speak to you. Remember, in Tarot it is much better to go with your own intuition than to take the word of another as truth just because they tell you they know more about it than you do. You decide. For those of you who have researched your definition, how did your intuitive definition compare to the commonly recognized meaning? Record below.

_____
_____
_____
_____
_____
_____
_____
_____

## Working Deeply with the Cards: An Example

The following is an example of the useful information you can get from a Tarot card when you work with it personally and directly vs. trying to memorize a set meaning.

This is a reading for myself I did several years ago about my life path. The question was: "What do I need to know at this point of my spiritual journey?" At the time, I was using the Rider Waite Smith deck. I drew the Fool.

The interpretation listed in the companion book for the Fool is new beginnings and innovative ideas. While I could identify with this definition to some extent, I felt it lacked the deeper interpretation and details that I was used to receiving from one of my readings. I then decided to use my normal method of working deeply with the details and symbols I saw within the card. The following is what I discovered:

## Example of Examining a Card Closely

Fool Upright, Rider Waite Smith Deck, Reading About Life Path:

List of the details I notice in the card:

- Person almost walking off of the cliff, head high, showing no worry of falling

- Yellow Sky

- White Sun

- Person's shirt sleeves look like wings (red) and various symbols on shirt

- White mountains in background

- White dog at Fool's feet as if to get his/her attention

- White rose in left hand

- A red hobo bag on a stick over his right shoulder

- Card number 0

- There is no snow on the cliff he/she is on, but there is snow on the mountains in background

- Green laurel wreath worn as a crown

This card reminds me of Kierkegaard's "Leap of Faith" philosophy that I studied in college. I see the Fool as the most confident and faith-filled person of the Tarot because he/she has the courage to move full speed ahead on his spiritual path, knowing full well he/she will not fall and that anything he encounters was meant to be. The Fool is someone who is innovative and doesn't allow the pack because he/she has the ability to connect to an inner knowing and doesn't need to follow the leader. The

Fool is not someone in the mainstream, nor can he truly be happy trying to live that way. He/she has evolved to the point where true inspiration comes from within.

The above interpretation, although highly personal, was also highly meaningful to me. It helped me think through my situation, open up my intuition and see things from my own unique perspective. In doing so, I discovered that it was not only the best card to answer my question, but because I had developed my own definition, I knew exactly where to go from there.

## Exercise 1E: Completing Your Work

Each and every time you study the cards or do a reading you should end your session with a formal completion process. This will keep you from feeling spacey or wired after the session and will make sure that what you have learned integrates more fully. In my experience, I have learned first hand how important this step can be. I often did readings by appointment at my metaphysical store, and I often needed to go from client to sales floor, especially when a client then wants assistance in making purchases. If I did not do a short grounding procedure, I simply could focus well enough to offer the assistance he or she really needed, and I would come across as a silly girl rather than a Tarot expert.

1) Start by taking a moment to acknowledge out loud or silently that you are done and to briefly acknowledge what you have learned from this particular working session.

2) Do the grounding exercise again. This time as you become aware of your body make sure that you release any extra energy you may have picked up during the reading that you do not need. An alternate option which I often do at the store is to quickly shuffle the deck, place them in their box, then rub my hands together to break the energetic connection between me and the deck.

3) Take a moment to re-focus on your space and express thanks for new insight. This is also a good time for prayers of gratitude to your spiritual guides if you feel so moved.

4) "Release your space" by undoing any physical modifications (blow out the candle, remove the do not disturb sign, tell the kids they can ask you questions now, etc.) As you are doing this make sure you are changing gears mentally. If you find that your memory is unusually bad this is a sign that you are not fully grounded and you need to go back and complete that step before you finish releasing your working space.

# Lesson Two
# The Minor Arcana & Simple Card Interpretation

- Archetype vs. Symbol
- The Skeletal Structure of a Tarot Deck
- Symbols & Archetypes in The Cards

# Symbols & Archetypes

Now that you have learned how to ground, set sacred space, and open up to your intuitive powers, you are ready to start a careful exploration of the cards themselves. Your major lesson of the cards is recognizing and analyzing symbols and archetypes. The distinction between the two is fuzzy for many, but it is one of the keys to really understanding what it is that is happening with the Tarot.

Briefly put, symbols represent things other than themselves. If you can think back to your literature studies in school you might remember that authors often used symbols to convey messages to the reader. Symbols, while widely recognized, can evoke different emotions from one person to the next. Symbols are typically agreed upon and refer to a specific meaning. Further, symbols are typically not cross-cultural. Take for example this symbol:($). Americans should all immediately know what I am referring to and even begin to have your own associations about your experience with $, how you feel about it, what you use it for, etc. You can even attach one single specific word as being more perfectly matched to the symbol $ than any other. For those who may not know, dollar is the word. This is true even though we will all quickly associate this with the broader concept of money.

The thing about $ is that it exists only as a form of communication. It is not actually the physical cash needed to pay for something, it is merely a character on my keyboard that I have created a number of associations for. You cannot draw $ on a piece of paper and expect to walk out of a store with merchandise. It represents a dollar but is not actually used in substitute of the dollar.

It is sometimes confusing to understand symbols because humans make everything into a symbol. Language is a symbol, as is art and fashion and most other aspects of the human experience. A key to understanding the place of symbols in Tarot is to remember that a symbol has only the meaning we bring to it and that is gained from our own experience. If I showed the symbol $ to an indigenous tribal person who had never encountered my culture she would not look at my symbol and nod wisely and then pull out similar symbols of her own while recounting past personal experience and spiritual tradition to me. However, if I were to show the same person an archetype that is exactly what would happen.

Archetypes are symbols that hold a spiritual and psychological energy that is so profound that they are immediately understood on an intuitive level by most people, people, regardless of the language they speak or what they are supposed to represent. In order to connect the symbol $ with the physical object of a dollar, one must be taught that the two objects belong together. However, there are some symbols that are universally understood. A skeleton for example needs no introduction to be connected to the concept of Death.

Archetypes are embodiments of forces and events that are so integrated into our human experience that they couldn't really be explained; they can only be experienced. The two most obvious examples of this are love and death.
It is fairly easy to teach a child of five or six what $ means and how to use it. Children are exceptionally open to symbolism and seem to grasp it quickly. If you show them the symbol $ and then a dollar they will connect the two. They can just as easily be taught to exchange physical dollars for something they want. But have you ever had to try and explain love or death to a child? There is a sense when doing so that although the child may grasp the fact, the meaning is impossible to communicate. In fact, many adults have a hard time fully understanding love or death. In order to understand the meaning, you must have first had the experience. This is why we are always telling children, "wait until you grow up and then you will understand." But is this an accurate statement? Do we truly learn this lesson as part of the maturing process, or is it just that as we age we have the experience and are changed by it?

Yet love and death are topics that humans frequently talk about. There are thousands of volumes of books on the subjects and they form the core of every major work of literature or art ever created, as they cross every cultural barrier we know. That is why we call these topics archetypal.

Carl Jung, a noted psychologist, talked about archetypes as coming from a collective unconscious shared by all humans. My personal experience would confirm this. Concepts like "Mother Earth" have an odd way of showing up in every place from butter commercials in the USA to religious rights in the Andes Mountains to Japanese literature. It is truly a Universal concept.

The prime distinction between symbols and archetypes is that anyone can be taught to understand the language of a particular symbol, but to understand an archetype you must undergo a personal psychological or spiritual experience. Both types of knowledge are important, and indeed vital to have in order to make your life's journey. Together they form the key to how the Tarot deck is structured, and the key to easily interpreting it.

## The Skeletal Structure of a Tarot Deck

The Tarot's first 22 cards, called the Major Arcana, rely on archetypes to convey their messages. These archetypes are essential to the human experience as all people encounter them at some point in their life. They are numbered and organized in a particular sequence that allows us to gather clues about how to further our own spiritual development by studying the patterns encoded in the sequence. (We will talk more about this in later chapters.) These archetypes form the spiritual guidebook of the journey of the soul. (Journey of the Fool)

The remainder of a Tarot deck is divided into four individual suits similar to our common playing cards and called the Minor Arcana. In fact, traditional playing cards are based on the Tarot and not the other way around. The Minor Arcana communicates its message through symbols and represent the ordinary, day to day realities that we must encounter along this journey. The symbols of the four suits each focus on a different area of life-skills and again are numbered and arranged in an order that gives us specific lessons to explore.

The Minor and Major Arcana together make up the traditional 78 card Tarot deck, and just by understanding this basic structure we can begin to gain information from a spread of Tarot cards, even if we do not know what the specific cards are "supposed" to mean.

## Symbols & Archetypes in the Cards

There is great value to knowing the traditions and meanings behind the symbols and archetypes in Tarot cards, but most students find that they learn more quickly and easily if they first explore what they already know about the Tarot. I promise you that you already know much more than you might think. That is the nature of symbols and archetypes, and therefore the nature of the Tarot.

In lesson one, we talked about the importance of preparing to do your readings by setting your workspace. This lesson will take that exercise one step further. It is probably best to read this lesson, including the examples all the way through before attempting to do the exercise. A word of caution: just reading this exercise will NOT work unless you actually do the physical work of the exercise. Learning the Tarot is about practice, not just reading a manual.

## Exercise 2A: Interpreting the Symbolism

>Find the notes you made for lesson one, the exercise of simply looking at a card and noting everything you see in it, and keep them at hand. If you have not done that exercise, stop and do it now, then proceed to this one. You can never be an accurate reader if you do not focus on each card, one at a time, symbol by symbol. This course will not work if you do not do every single assignment in its sequence. This is not busy work but purposeful lessons arranged to help you master the Tarot. Doing these exercises can bring startling revelations and can, in and of itself, enable you to do simple and accurate readings.

>Once you have the notes you made listing everything you noticed in a single card, take a moment to review the steps in lesson one and prepare to do a reading. Remember the steps for preparing to work psychically are:

1) ***Preparing Mentally:*** Make sure that you are in a good frame of mind to work. Make sure you are not unduly emotional in any one direction, are not under the influence of drugs, alcohol, or any substance that may impair judgment, and that you are focused on the goal of psychic development.

2) ***Establish your Working Space***: Make sure that you have time and a comfortable place with no distractions in which to work. Go one step farther by ensuring that you create a sense of "holy ground" where you are working. Rituals from your spiritual practice and/or the use of focusing objects like candles or crystals are appropriate for this step and can be very helpful.

3) ***Sensing Energy***: Allow yourself to activate the mental "on" switch for psychic perception. Take a moment to feel (or just imagine what you think it would feel like if you are not yet able to do this) the flow of energy in the universe. Again, you may choose to bolster this ability through any personal rituals you find helpful.

4) ***Grounding:*** This is vitally important. Make sure that you have a channel (or imagine one) that takes excess or unwanted energy into the earth.

After you have done this, take out your notes from the last exercise. (You really should keep a Tarot Journal in addition to taking notes in this book.) Start this exercise by marking the time and date and the name of the card you worked with last time and whether it was a Major or Minor Arcana card.

How do you know whether it is Major or Minor Arcana card? Remember that the deck is divided into five main sections. There are four suits of the Minor Arcana similar to the suits in a regular deck of playing cards - the Swords, the Wands, the Cups and the Pentacles. In addition to these you will find the Major Arcana, all of which have titles in boldface under the picture. So, for example, anything that is numbered with a suit name appearing in its title is part of the Minor Arcana, such as The Seven of Swords and the Three of Pentacles. Death and Temperance are Major Arcana cards because their title appears at the bottom in boldface, and their card numbers are not followed by a suit name. To further help you out, most decks will also number Major Arcana with Roman Numerals on the top ranging from 0 (The Fool) to XXI (The World).

Once you have noted whether you have a Minor or Major Arcana Card, remove it from the deck and put the other cards away. Without looking at your notes from last time, notice as much detail in the card as you can. Just by looking at the picture, what type of story do you think the card might be telling? If you were there what time of day would it be? What time of year does it look like? What types of activity (or non-activity) are going on in the card? What do you think any of the characters in the card would be like if you were to meet them? Does it remind you of an instance in real or fictional life that resonates with you? What symbols stand out? When you look away from the card, what mood or visuals linger?

Just let whatever comes to you come, and do not try to hinder or enhance your personal insight. Even if you think it is only your imagination talking, that's fine. Let it talk. The only way to tap into your intuition is to let it flow without boundaries. You might be pleasantly surprised what you uncover.

Write down your impressions. There are no wrong answers to this exercise. Just make note of your personal "sense" of the card.

Now take a look at your notes from last time and look for the specific details and/or objects you noticed in the card. For example, if you chose the five of pentacles, some of the things you may have written down are: snow, a stained-glass window, crutches, nighttime, ragged clothes, barefoot, a broken leg.

Now choose the three symbols that stand out most to you and focus on those for the time being. Let's say you have chosen the stained-glass window, the crutches, and the snow.

Take a moment to study these specific symbols and try to pinpoint the most common tangible experiences you can think of. Where is one likely to see a stained-glass window? Why is it that you use crutches? How would it feel to be walking around barefoot in a snowstorm? Being able to really learn Tarot and offer consistent readings is being able to have on hand easily understandable experiences that most can identify with.

Write down your observations and then read on to find out why this simple exercise in observation can make you a Tarot expert.

_____
_____
_____
_____
_____
_____
_____
_____
_____
_____
_____

If you review what you have written about your impressions when meditating on the card, and combine that with your associations with concrete symbols, you will find that you can easily put the two together to form a meaningful definition for the card. Take a moment to do this, and in a few moments, you will have your very own definition of the 5 of pentacles.

What time of day, and what time of year do you think it is in the five of pentacles? Let's say middle of the night in winter. Further study might lead one to feel that the characters are very tired and are on some type of journey, most likely to seek help.

When one looks at the individual symbols in the card very literally and very narrowly one might observe that crutches are used by someone who cannot stand on their own two feet, stained glass is most commonly found in churches and snow makes traveling difficult. Also, their barefoot condition is very likely hampering not only their journey, but indicating how their journey has gone so far. It may also indicate financial difficulties.

When all the information is put together this image paints a fairly full picture, and it is easy to see why some of the standard interpretations for the five of pentacles include:

*Physical/emotional/spiritual loss
*Destitution, Bankruptcy, Failure
*Homelessness
*Lack of preparation
*Feeling alone, abandonment
*Life lesson(s) that must be learned   independently

**The Five of Pentacles**

These meanings, and ones like them, are found in many "standard" Tarot books. Tarot teachers often instruct you to pick a single word that reminds you of this card and commit it to memory as a way to learn the meanings of the cards. Using this method, many people would choose, "loss, "sorrow", "poverty", etc.

Besides being hopelessly depressing, these meanings are simply far less accurate than the meaning you can gain by working with what you have written in your Journal.

Let me show you. Suppose you are doing a reading on the question: "Will I get a new job soon?"

If you were to do a reading on this question, and the five of pentacles is drawn, from traditional meanings you would likely come out with a simple no and that would be the end of it. Makes sense, right? But as we all know it can be terrifying to be poor and out of work and no human is going to be satisfied, or much aided for that matter with a simple no for an answer. The cards are more than a yes/no answering machine; they are a system of spiritual information and guidance. Do not limit them in their help to you or your clients.

To demonstrate this, take a moment to pick a question that is on your mind, and try to think of the follow questions that you would like to know regarding this question. Write them all down.

Human nature will lead you to the next series of obvious questions. "Well when will I get a job?" And "How am I supposed to support myself?" And "But what about my family and other obligations?"

Using the observations, you made earlier, these questions can be answered easily. We noted that people on crutches cannot support themselves and that churches have stained glass, right? Well one interpretation could be that support (crutches) and spiritual sanctuary are needed.

We might combine this with the journey theme we picked up on to advise the client (or our self) that it is important on this spiritual journey to not look for a job but instead look for some type of assistance (crutch). We might further observe that they are in need of some type of healing because they, perhaps like the characters on the card, cannot stand on their own two feet. We might also see however that this is not the right time to move forward in the job search right now (the snow can represent obstacles) but obstacles, like snow, are temporary and soon enough a new opportunity will come. Depending on the season we might even tell the client that a job prospect will likely come in the springtime if you want to interpret the snow as a seasonal marker. When asked about the family, we might find that the family is going to take the lead in curing the situation and not the other way around.

This last sentence was obtained by noticing that the associations we were working with placed the questioner, as the person with the broken leg in the picture (because we decided the crutch was one of the primary symbols.) Once this is done then we can take new questions about the situation such as, "What about my family", and look again at the picture and focus. In this case the other person in the picture looks to be leading or in front of the person with the crutches and there is a "feeling" of connection or family.

## An Intuitive Meaning for the 5 of Pentacles

Support and spiritual sanctuary are needed. Now is the time to seek healing and learn to receive support from others. More options and mobility will come in time. Someone will come to help you find the material resources you need and are leading the way to your solution right now. Trying to go it alone will throw you off balance and cause hardship, disharmony and struggle.

Now take the meaning you have made for yourself and combine it with your observations and follow up questions to create a more specific answer. Write it down.

This type of synthesis of observations can lead to a great deal of specific information. It is also highly personal. Someone who has been homeless will have his or her own personal connections to the card, as will someone who has at one point been the guide for another in this situation.

I cannot stress enough that the Tarot is ultimately an intuitive art, and adding our individual set of symbols and personal circumstances will transform you from a Tarot reader to a Tarot expert. Our personal observations can be very powerful and more accurate than a traditional meaning out of a book.

In a few days read over what you have written and review what question you associated your meaning with. Decide for yourself if it seems accurate. Chances are you will be pleasantly surprised.

Once you have completed this exercise be sure to take a moment to allow yourself to imagine any excess or unwanted emotions or energy to flow into the earth. Take a few deep breaths and imagine that the breaths are filling you with fresh, healing and cleansing energies. Respectfully release your sacred space and consciously change mental gears back into everyday focus.

# Lesson Three
# The Suit of Swords

- The Four Symbols of the Minor Arcana
- The Symbolic History of Swords and Their Meanings
- Swords in Art and Literature
- Contemporary Customs and Traditions around Swords
- Swords and the Element of Air
- Swords in Religion
- Significance of Swords in a Reading
- Expanding Your Personal Understanding of Swords

## The Four Symbolic Suits of the Minor Arcana

Once we have begun to open up our psychic process and relate to the cards from an intuitive perspective, it is time to add specific knowledge about the traditional meanings and history of the symbolism in the cards.

While one could spend a lifetime studying the symbolism of different cards and different decks, there is an underlying symbolic structure that is consistent from deck to deck. Once you understand this basic symbolism you will be able to do a basic reading with any traditional 78 card Tarot deck even if you have never seen it before.

The symbolism in the Minor Arcana is the starting point. As we have discussed before, the Minor Arcana is divided into four basic Suits much like playing cards which are a descendent of the Tarot. The four suits are:

**SWORDS**: sometimes called knives, daggers, or blades

**WANDS**: also called rods, staves, batons, or spears

**CUPS**: also called bowls, chalices, grails, cauldrons, or vessels

**PENTACLES**: also called stones, crystals, coins, or

disks

Each suit is symbolic of a whole category of meaning and is associated with an element (air, fire, water, or earth) as well as with such things as psychological outlook, physical occupation, and social positioning. In addition, each suit symbol has a long mythological and cultural history with tales in the oral traditions telling of an object of magical powers that corresponds to each of the suits of the Major Arcana.

The important thing to know about these traditions is that it is a waste of your time, especially in the early stages of your Tarot training, to memorize all of the associations or "correspondences" for each of the suits.

Memorizing the correspondences does not work for two reasons:

1) Recalling memorized material stops the intuitive process, and
2) If you do not have a full understanding of the meaning behind a correspondence it is useless in a reading anyway.

So, relax. You do not have to memorize anything. A card's true meaning for you will manifest all on its own through your regular practices. So, how does one begin to develop insight as to a card's meaning? Read the following material a few times and think about it. See which bits capture your imagination and which bits fit with your personal experience. Then do the exercises at the end of the lesson. You may want to re-read this information from time to time but you will find that by simply working with it you will quickly begin to understand it and recall it without effort. True knowledge is different than recalling something memorized, and in no way develops intuition. Be patient with the process and be open to what comes, and you will be amazed at the results.

## The Symbolic History of Swords and Their Meanings

Swords have been in use for thousands of years and many customs and traditions have sprung up around their manufacture and use. Since the Tarot truly took hold during the Renaissance in Italy we will base most of our look at sword history and customs on the traditions of Europe from 1000 ACE to 1700 ACE.

One of the most important things to remember about the suit of Swords is that Swords are not depicted solely as weapons.

Many cultures looked upon swords as magical, especially the crafting of swords. In order to forge a sword, all four elements are used. The metal itself is from the earth, air is essential for keeping the bellows going in order to make the fire hot enough to shape the sword, and water is used in the cooling and tempering process. Because of this, the art of the blacksmith was considered magical and the crafting of a sword particularly so.

While it was recognized that the magical mixing of elements was involved with almost any form of blacksmithing, swords were seen as requiring particular magical skill for a few reasons:

1) The art of forming a sword that is both hard enough to hold a good edge and flexible enough not to break required specific knowledge and skill. This knowledge was often kept secret and handed down in families as a prized heirloom.

2) Crafting a sword requires considerably more time and effort than crafting a horseshoe or a spearhead, so it was reserved either for times of great need or great luxury.

3) Swords were particularly effective weapons in an era when minor skirmishes and wars were simply a matter of life. When the spring came, so did the chance of war, so having a sword on hand increased the odds of making it through the summer to the next harvest.

4) Swords have always been associated with the upper class and with the traditions of chivalry and political hierarchy. Because of this they have been surrounded with countless rituals of honor and belonging.

5) Most towns that had their own blacksmith tended to think of themselves as being either unusually prosperous, unusually lucky, or both. Towns (and cultures or tribes for that matter) that were known for having blacksmiths who could make high quality swords were unusually important and powerful in the political landscape of the time. Owning a sword was considered to be a sign of wealth and political power.

During the Renaissance, there were very strict laws throughout most of Europe pertaining to who was allowed to own a sword and under what circumstances they were allowed to use it. In order to own a sword openly a person had to be of a noble class and usually in service to a Feudal Lord. Swords were very, very expensive and typically were handed down from father to son.

Swords were often an indication of being of the knight and warrior class. In fact, you could not be a knight unless you owned a sword. When a man was first given his sword he typically stayed up all night and prayed over it, and also took a vow of loyalty to his King or other overlord. These vows were sometimes filled with the chivalry we see in the movies but they were more often a political agreement to provide their Lord services as a warrior in exchange for lands and freedom. The oath, however, was absolutely binding. The very fact that a person carried a sword was a signal to others that he had taken service with one particular Lord or another and was sworn to uphold the political aims of that Lord to the death, whether he agreed with that Lord or not. It was very common for the sword's scabbard to bear some mark indicating to what Lord or country the particular knight was bound. Swords were not weapons of mass destruction or objects up for sale, but rather something that was earned.

While it is perfectly possible to pick up a staff or spear and get fairly good at using it just by play fighting with one's fellows, swords are another matter and require extensive training to use. If you do not train, chances are that in your first fight you will trip over yourself and have the sword fed to you by your opponent.

This type of training takes time and access to a teacher or swordmaster. This is another reason that swords were associated with the higher classes. Only a noble could afford to take his son out of the fields or the workshops in order to allow him the hours of practice it took to become proficient with a sword. This required training in logistics, mathematics for troop deployment, strategy, and the various forms of warfare technology of the day. It is also important to note that during much of the Renaissance it was as important to follow the forms of correct warfare as it was to be good at fighting.

During the European Renaissance, the class a person held also indicated their job description. Their class dictated what they were allowed to do and not do, where they could go and under what circumstances, and what they were allowed to learn and not learn. As you can see from the outline of customs mentioned here, the ownership and use of a sword led to a very particular lifestyle. As with any lifestyle certain experiences and values became more important than others, and it is from these attitudes that we get the "traditional meanings" for the suit of Swords.

## Swords in Art and Literature

The myth that most clearly embodies the nuances of swords is the myth of King Arthur. This is not only because his journey hinges around Excalibur and the sword he pulled out of the stone in later myths. (Note: originally these actually were different swords and not one and the same!) King Arthur mostly embodies the mystery of the sword because of his quest for "truth and justice"; his significant political effect on the land and the tremendous mental energy embodied in essentially rewriting the rules of knighthood and chivalry.

## Contemporary Customs and Traditions

Mostly swords are associated with the realm of ideas and ideological loyalties. Honor and duty were vastly more important than family or personal opinion. In a world where the majority of people never ventured more than fifteen miles from their homes, knights traveled into far distant lands (remember the Crusades?) and risked their very lives for points of theology, politics and honor. It was "what they were sworn to uphold" or "what they were fighting for" that became the most important factor in their lives.

In addition, swords have a strong association with heredity, hierarchical structure, and with thinking and planning. There is also a strong sense that you need to be clear headed and unemotional. While most people think of war as emotional and irrational (and while the causes of almost all wars are certainly intertwined with pure irrational stupidity) the fact of the matter is that to stay alive in a war you must remain calm and think clearly. This is particularly true in an age where bombs did not really exist and one's opponent was a mere arm's length away.

In modern times swords are associated with writing and business. This makes sense if you think about it. Modern day corporations are the replacement of the old city-states and tribes vying for economic and political positioning. Lawyers are in many ways the swordsmen of today. They are under strict contract with their employer whose interest they purportedly serve, while they also have an ethical oath to justice and the modern-day equivalents of chivalry.

## Swords and the Element of Air

Swords are also associated with the element of air. While it is true that they have a strong connection to all of the elements (as stated above) air is chosen for two main reasons:

1) The intense mental functions associated with Swords are usually associated with air.

2) While a sword is made of all of the elements, its power is to bring air into contact with whatever it cuts. If you cut a fruit in two with a knife you immediately let air into where there had been none before.

## Swords in Religion

It might be startling to believe, but swords have been used as a major symbol in many of the world's major religions. In fact, almost every religion believes that the sword is a tool for cutting illusion and therefore represents courage, intelligence, and reason. While this is by no means a thorough list, below are a few examples for your reference.

1) In Buddhism, the sword represents wisdom. The Bodhisattva Manjusri, who embodies wisdom, is often depicted wielding a sword, sometimes five-pointed. Wisdom is the sword that cuts away illusion and brings in awareness. The sword of wisdom cuts once, decisively, and then continues its process of cutting.

2) The Kabbalah is a Hebrew mystical tradition that is gaining in popularity today. As with all mystical traditions, the purpose of the Kabbalah is to provide humanity with an experience of God. The word itself, KBL means, "to receive." The most important feature of the Kabbalah is a glyph called the Tree of Life.

    In the Kabbalah, God, the Unknowable, is referred to as the Ain Soph. The universe is the garment in which Ain Soph manifests itself. This garment is called the sephiroth, in which there are ten in number. The sephiroth are referred to as intelligences, radiations, emanations, principles, powers, worlds, and/or organs of God. The ten sephiroth of the Tree of Life are in the same order that creation manifested. When this zigzag path is traced on the glyph, Kabbalists refer to it as the Sacred or Flaming Sword.

3) The Athame, a sacred blade in Wiccan and Pagan traditions, is a knife or sword that represents the element of air. This blade is used in the moderate direction of energy, is purely ceremonial in nature, and contrary to popular belief is never used for cutting or sacrifice. The Athame is double edged, representing the male and female duality of nature.

4) The Khanda is the symbol of the Sikhs, as the Cross is to Christians or the Star of David is to Jews. The symbol derives its name from the double-edged sword (also called a Khanda) which appears at the center of the logo. This double-edged sword is a metaphor of Divine Knowledge, with its sharp edges cleaving Truth from Falsehood. The right edge of the double-edged sword symbolizes freedom and authority governed by moral and spiritual values. The sides emphasize the equal emphasis that a Sikh must place on spiritual aspirations as well as obligations to society.

5) There are also many referencing in the Bible that depict the sword as a symbol of air and spirit rather than a cutting tool or weapon.

"And take the helmet of salvation, and the sword of the spirit, which is the word of God" Ephesians 6:17

"For the word of God is living and powerful and sharper than any two-edged sword, piercing even to the division of soul and spirit, and of joints and marrow, and is a discerner of the thoughts and intents of the heart" Hebrews 4:12

Paramhansa Yogananda, a great saint of India, taught the boys at his Ranchi school the use of the sword as a metaphor of right mind and right action. When I opened my holistic center in 2003, I named it The Sacred Sword in honor of many of the above references.

## Significance of Swords in A Reading

Questions to ask yourself when interpreting Sword cards are: What is the plan or strategy? Who else has gone through a similar situation, and how do I get information from him or her about what to do? Do I have all the information I need? What ideals are important to adhere to in this situation? What has been (or should be) put into writing? What is the honorable course of action? What is it I am trying to win and how will I know when I have won it?

## Expanding Your Personal Understanding of Swords

For more insight into the symbol of the sword, watch the movies Braveheart, and/or The Last Samurai, read Shakespeare's Henry V, or learn the history of Excalibur/King Arthur.

# Lesson Four
# The Minor Arcana: Wands and Cups

- The Symbolic History of Wands and Their Meanings
- Wands in Art and Literature
- Contemporary Customs and Traditions around Wands
- Wands and the Element of Fire
- Significance of Wands in a Reading
- Expanding Your Personal Understanding of Wands
- The Symbolic History of Cups and Their Meanings
- Cups in Art and Literature
- Contemporary Customs and Traditions around Cups
- Cups and the Element of Water
- Significance of Cups in a Reading
- Expanding Your Personal Understanding of Cups

# The Symbolic History of Wands and Their Meanings

Just as the Swords have their rich history, so too is there is a tradition of magic surrounding the suit of Wands. Wands are intimately associated with trees and the forest and the many traditions surrounding both. While wands are clearly tools (such as a walking stick or a hoe or a spear) it is important to remember that they are, like everything else in the Tarot, much more than what they appear.

One of the first things we need to cover to really understand the Wands is to realize that unlike the Swords, the Wands are a bit harder to define. In the deck, Wands show up as different things with different uses, whereas the Swords always look the same. For example, Wands in various cards in the sequence have been depicted as hoes, spears, arrows, longbows, walking staves, batons, pikes and flagpoles. Some decks also show them as blooming with flower buds in the higher numbers. As such, this is often the hardest suit for the beginner to approach due to their versatility.

Nevertheless, the first question we ask about Wands is the same as the first question we asked about Swords. In the time and place of Renaissance Europe how did one acquire and use a wand? Unlike the status and/or wealth required to own a sword, all one needed to acquire a wand was to simply go into the forest and cut yourself a branch. There is magic and tradition around this, but magic and tradition of a different kind. During the Renaissance period, not every village had a blacksmith or access to one, but almost all towns had at least some access to trees. The raw materials for wands in their many guises were therefore easy to come by, and required far less skill to create and use. It was the empowering of the wand and understanding its use as a tool that was the magical process connected to it rather than its manufacture.

Take for example the process of learning to hunt with a bow. This is a skill that requires the understanding of air and wind and how that will affect the shot, but it also requires understanding fire in the indirect form of the passion and vitality of whatever you are hunting. There is a lot of energy and motion involved in using the wand or arrow. The interesting thing about this process is that while you are forging a sword you direct each of the elements towards a particular use, but when you are forming a bow or arrow the elements are present but subordinate to your skill.

Another example is the simple walking staff. Getting one is no problem, as almost everyone has found or made their own on a hike, even today. Owning one is and was no difficult feat, and to the best of my knowledge there has never been laws about who could own a walking staff. But what about using one?

In Renaissance Europe (and to some degree today) there were two primary ways one used a walking staff. The first way was used as a cane and the second way is that he or she went on prolonged journeys. In the particular time and place we are talking about, traveling and journeying was not the typical mode of activity, and contrary to popular belief most of the populace did not live long enough to need a cane to walk with. Therefore, a trusted walking staff was not the type of thing everyone used. It was the type of thing anyone could use, but as a practical matter wise people most commonly used it.

This wisdom was most often gained by going on pilgrimages or by attaining wisdom through age. Pilgrims who often traveled across wild country in many cases were clergy or people with an understanding of plant medicines. Almost all old people of the time had learned plant medicine as it was the only mode of healing available. In either case the wisdom of the day was wrapped up in herb and nature lore. In fact, one could not expect to live very long on a pilgrimage or even at home in the village without the benefit of herbal remedies.

The walking staff would be used in the process of gathering herbs and food in several ways. It obviously would offer support, making travel through wild places easier. It would also serve as protection from wild critters, and allow its user to knock nuts or fruit off of high tree tops. It could serve as an impromptu shovel for digging up plants, and in some cases, serve as either a place marker or a map itself. (The Celts had a complex language that was made by putting notches on a staff and many other peoples in Europe had similar if less sophisticated systems.) In short, the staff was so useful that all pilgrims and herbalists had one, and the staff even became a mark of their societal rank and job description in the same way that swords would define knights. In fact, many decks depict a flowering staff for this reason.

Herbology, like hunting, requires a synthesis of the elements. Many medicinal plants are recognized by their smell which is air, in some cases cooking which is fire, and the type and quality of plants available depend heavily on what water (rainfall) is about, and herbs themselves are from the earth. Most of all, all of this knowledge must be used together in order to use the plants correctly. So just as with the activity of hunting, the activity of gathering requires an experiential knowledge of how the elements work together as a unit.

These two examples, the hunting bow and the pilgrims' staff, show us how wands take their power from the magical understanding of how they are used. This also is a type of knowledge based on personal experience. It is not handed down from father to son, and it is not acquired through formal training. It is rather a matter of trial and error, practice, and the collective wisdom of the community. Unlike sword fighting and politics which were areas of knowledge closely guarded, hunting and gathering knowledge is shared. A pilgrim might learn of one herb's properties from one person in one town and another herb's properties from a different person in a different town. Learning where to hunt was similar.

Although one might have a mentor who shared certain knowledge, the fruits of the hunt were often shared with extended family and community. This means if someone discovered a particularly good hunting spot, it would be shared freely.

So,, what are Wands telling us? Remember that in the Tarot the individual symbols work to remind us about particular areas of human development and orientation. What does the particular set of experiences associated with the Wands tell us about the class, job descriptions, mobility, learning, and other environmental factors that shaped the people who used them? When we understand these things, we understand what "truths" about human nature and experience the Wands are representing in the Tarot. Wands, since they are connected to hunting, gathering, and farming are associated with the peasant class and with rural communities.

Wands also represent extended community. Just as a pilgrim is a member of a religious community seeking further enlightenment, the hunters and wise people of the day were respected members of their local communities. In both cases what was gained on the journey, whether it is medicine, knowledge, or food, was shared.

Pilgrims, bards, and tradesmen who brought their crafts from town to town also brought news. In a period where there were no newspapers, TVs, radios, or Internet connections, these travelers were considered the main source of information. As such they were naturally seen as authority figures on many things. Certainly, the herbalists and wise people of the day were authority figures and in some areas were THE authority figure. This authority did not however come from anyone else. It was not authority granted to them by a licensing body, a school, a boss, or a political figure. It was authority that came directly from their own life experiences because they had been there and knew first hand what they were talking about.

Wands are also associated with traveling and with apprenticeships and any period of learning from hands-on personal experience, as well as with community transformation. When a bard or pilgrim came to town, the community was changed and transformed by the news and contact this person brought from the outside world. A local farmer or hunter could certainly transform life for everyone in the community through a particularly good crop or successful hunt. Likewise, the local herbalist or wise person was to help heal the community when needed and to offer the benefit of his or her life experience to help the community make it through the day to day lessons and transformations that life, love, and death in a close community brings.

## Wands in Art and Literature

One of the best examples of the mythology and magical traditions around the wand is the story of Robin Hood. His very tag line "stole from the rich and gave to the poor" clearly indicates his association with the peasant class. His Merry Men and Marian are a clear reminder of the importance of community and of his role as the authority in that community. And finally, the stories about his clever tricks for besting the sheriff point out that his power comes from his own experiences and nothing else.

## Contemporary Customs and Traditions

Although we do not have the same type of pilgrims and herbalists we once did, there are plenty of traditions alive and well that involves wands. The phrase "passing the wand" or "passing the torch" is still used to describe when one community leader passes on leadership to another. In addition, things such as talking sticks, rain sticks, and even totem poles seem to have found a place in the hearts of contemporary humans.

## Wands and the Element of Fire

The key element associated with Wands is Fire. The association with fire comes from three sources:

1) Photosynthesis. Wands are made of wood, and one of the most remarkable things about wood and all forms of plant life is their unique ability to turn sunlight (fire) into useable energy. Other types of living things cannot perform this miracle. Wood simply has a natural affinity with fire because it easily catches on fire.

2) The sheer passion and life force that working with wands requires and enhances is a quality of Fire. If you think about it, you have to be pretty passionate to wander around the countryside as a pilgrim, and the passion or "thrill of the hunt" is a well-known experience. Likewise farming or herb crafting takes a real creative passion to excel at.

3) Just as swords can bring air by cutting, wands bring fire via torches, matches, kindling, and fire logs, just as cups aid in transporting water and pentacles in transporting earth.

## Significance of Wands in a Reading

Questions to ask yourself when Wands show up in a reading are: How are my current experiences shaping and teaching me right now? What am I passionate about, and what do I desire? What am I an authority on, and how can I use the sense of confidence and security that authority gives me in this particular situation? How can I draw on my community for support and how is my personal question representative of the types of transformations going on throughout my community? What is the first step on my new journey of self-awareness?

## Expanding Your Personal Understanding of Wands

To gain more insight into Wands you may want to watch Robin Hood, or The Lord of The Rings trilogy (pay special attention to Gandalf).

## The Symbolic History of Cups and Their Meanings

Throughout ancient history and well into the late Middle Ages and early Renaissance, the cauldron and its later symbolic equivalent the cup or chalice was the primary symbol of home's hearth and personal magic. Like the sword and the wand, the cauldron was associated with a particular element (water) but was also understood to have a magical relationship with all elements. The cauldron was often the only metal object a poor family might own, and as such was an important symbol of the earth (earth associations were also gained from the herbs and meat often inside the cauldron.) In addition, it was placed over a fire, and the scent from whatever was cooking was thought to carry the magic from the cauldron through the air. Cauldrons and cups are also an obvious vessel for water.

Where the sword is formed of the elements and the wand is empowered by the elements, the cauldron or cup is used for mixing the elements together. Food, medicines, and even poisons were made in the cauldron or drunk from a cup, and it was the knowledge of how to appropriately combine the ingredients or elements that gave the power to whatever was brewing.

While everyone probably owned a drinking cup during this period of history, not everyone owned their own cooking vessel. Typically, families had one main cauldron and the eldest female of the household oversaw this. It would then be her job to make sure that there was always food of some kind in the cauldron. Unlike modern times where food can be obtained easily, acquiring food was a long, drawn out, time consuming event from growing to gathering to preparation. In an era where there were no refrigerators, canned and jarred goods, or deliveries from other lands, food became an important symbol of life force, social status, and faith.

It is this connection between the cauldron and faith (faith that the mother earth will provide enough to feed the family) that led to the connection in early Renaissance between the mythological symbolism of the cauldron and that of the Holy Grail. The cauldron had figured prominently in pre-Christian myths as the symbol of regeneration, abundance, and spiritual transformation. It was also associated with the Mother Goddess (often referred to as her womb) and was thought of as the prime source of physical and spiritual healing as well as a gateway to connection with the Gods. As Christianity became a dominant force in Europe, and the custom of Communion and the religious symbolism behind it took hold, the parallels between the cauldron and the cup from the Last Supper became obvious. A merging of the two traditions created the myths and traditions of the Holy Grail.

The stories of the Holy Grail and of the various knights who went in search of it were a significant cultural force in the shaping of European History. These myths or "Romances" as they became known had a major impact on the symbolism and ideas within the Tarot.

One of the major effects that the grail myths had was to firmly connect the contemporary Church to the old Pagan traditions of healing through herbs, or the sacred wells, mystical visions, and Holy Communion. Despite the biblical history behind the practice of Communion, it is doubtful that it would have taken as strong a hold in Europe as it did if there were not elements of familiarity for the people being converted. Communion was one of these main elements.

This background is important to know if we are going to ask our standard Tarot question of this symbol. Who had a cup/cauldron, and how did having and using one shape their experience and outlook?

While it was still true that almost every household had some type of cauldron, during the Renaissance it became true that grails were seen as the province of the Church. One of the things used to distinguish grails from other vessels was the shape. Common people typically had drinking horns, cups, bowls, cauldron pots, and tumblers, and minor nobility had wide bowls like goblets. Grails shaped like wineglasses were more common as part of Church regalia or in the hands of high ranking nobles who where supposed to be God's emissaries on earth. Clergy not only had the ability to use herbs for healing and spiritual endeavors, but also knew how to make poison when the time was needed.

The cups are also associated with love; whether it is the mother who tends to the cauldron or the Church's hand in birth and marriage ceremonies. The Church did a great deal of marriage counseling as it were and was often heavily involved in the marriage decisions of their flock. In addition, the whole idea of "family" was seen as an ordered extension of God's plan and the various obligations of family members to one another were seen as handed down by God. Remember that men and women in many religious institutions of the day were (and still are) called Father, Brother, Sister and Mother.

Another interesting thing to note is that during this period of history most people were illiterate, but clergymen often could read and write in several languages. Other than the nobles, the clergy was the only class to be given what we currently think of as an education. This has great bearing on the Cups and the Tarot.

The nobles used their reading and writing primarily for political and organizational affairs and for correspondence. However, the clergy was involved in the study of the classical writings and with philosophy. Almost all philosophical writings from this period are intertwined with theological concerns and written by members of the Church. Cups then have a connection to a life of philosophical inquiry, spiritual, and theological exploration.

In addition to traditional clergy, the midwife of the Renaissance would be highly associated with the Cup and its powers. During this time there were almost no regular doctors as we know them, so the midwife's role was significant. She would provide practical and spiritual nurturing to families and entire villages, as well as the healing and teaching roles associated with the job of helping a mother give birth. In many rural areas the midwife would take on some or all of the duties on that became associated with the Church. Vessels and cauldrons were the symbol of the Midwife and a major part of her regular work as she brewed teas and tinctures and healing aids for the mother, washed and cleaned newborns, and fed the new mother.

Cups in the Tarot have strong associations with emotional and spiritual transformation. Their connection to family and to both mundane and spiritual love is a strong theme, as is their connection to healing and nurturing. In some cases, Cups can also represent the darker aspects of death or deceit as with the use of poison or the risks associated with childbirth and healing during a time of high mortality.

## Cups in Art and Literature

Perhaps the most appropriate myth for the suit of Cups is that of Tristan and Isolde, however as it is not as well known now as it was 100 years ago I suggest you think of Romeo and Juliet. This play is almost entirely about Cup themes. The aspect of love is of course present. Equally present are the ideas of family and obligation to family, and of personal and spiritual transformation. The fate of the lovers forces transformation on their respective houses, but they are also seeking their own emotional and spiritual transformations throughout the play. As they seek to find a way to be together (with the help of a Mother figure in the nurse and a clergyman) they are also seeking to understand themselves and where they fit in the world both emotionally and spiritually.

## Contemporary Customs and Traditions

In contemporary society, we still have clergy who use cups in Communion and perform duties that might be said to have Cup energy. We also have psychologists, artists, coaches, and "cultural creatives" that do the same thing. The idea of the cup has been expanded into the idea of a circle or a sacred container.

## Cups and the Element of Water

The Suit of Cups is associated with water because of a cup's fluidity and tendency to fill the shape it is in. Water has long been associated with emotion and spiritual feeling. In its most basic aspect, cups, cauldrons, and other vessels allow humans to transport water. Where there is a sense with both Swords and Wands that the tool can "cause to appear or make" the element- with cups it is a matter of making the element bend to human needs.

## Significance of Cups in a Reading

Questions to ask yourself when you encounter cups in a spread are: What emotions are affecting the situation? How are my family and close loved ones playing into the situation? What am I seeking in terms of personal and spiritual fulfillment? What needs to be healed? How can I gain or give nurturing?

## Expanding Your Personal Understanding of Cups

If you are interested in getting a further understanding of Cups I suggest you read: Tristan & Isolde, or read (or watch films based on) the myth of the Holy Grail. For those of you new to the grail myth, any adaptation of the story of Perceval (sometimes spelled Parseval) would be fun and informative.

# Lesson Five
# Pentacles and Minor Arcana Correspondences

- The Symbolic History of Pentacles and Their Meanings
- Pentacles in Art and Literature
- Contemporary Customs and Traditions About Pentacles
- Pentacles and the Element of Earth
- Significance of Pentacles in A Reading
- Expanding Your Personal Understanding of Pentacle
- Minor Arcana Correspondence - Traditional Meanings
- Minor Arcana Correspondence Chart- Mythology

## The Symbolic History of Pentacles and Their Meanings

Pentacles are associated with the earth and things of the earth. If you cut an apple in half you will find that the seeds form a star shape, surrounded by the circle of the fruit itself. The actual physical object of the pentacle is most often a coin or a medallion. Coins and medallions are made of metal that is earth itself. However, like the sword, a coin or a medallion had to be minted or shaped. This process engaged all the elements just as it did with a sword. Thus, the pentacle has a magical association with all of the elements just like the sword but it is particularly a symbol of earth.

During the Middle Ages, the merchants and the wealthy exchanged money. No one else really used money, and necessities were obtained via the barter of goods. Medallions and jewelry as we understand them today were not easily accessible to the common person. Church and political officials wore metal jewelry as much as a sign of their rank as for adornment. Anyone who was not a merchant, of the higher class, or a member of the Church would simply not have access to many coins or bits of jewelry during the normal course of events.

As with the sword, the restricted access to coinage and jewelry caused certain laws and customs to spring up around the pentacle. The first set of customs revolved around the pentacle design itself, the five-pointed star. While this is seen by some in modern times as a negative sign or a sign of Satanists, that is not the real use or meaning of the pentacle symbol today, and was not even a remote possibility during the Middle Ages. (Satanism as we understand it today did not really spring up until the very late Renaissance).

The design of the five-pointed star was both a reference to abundant crops, as it was a common symbol for apple crops and other fruit bearing crops, as well as a sign of good luck and healing that was carried out of the Near East during the Crusades. It was therefore used as a dual symbol of protection and abundance and can be found on many medieval churches. The protective and lucky aspects of the symbol made it a popular mark and it was occasionally used on the back of coins for this reason. The very fact that pentacles were objects of a certain rarity enhanced their use as magical objects and good luck objects.

Money and coins had a host of interesting customs surrounding its use during the Middle Ages. One of the most notable is the Church belief that it was a sin to gain interest for loaning money. This practice, called usury, forms the fabric of modern fiscal arrangements but was strictly forbidden by the Catholic Church (which was at that time the only Christian Church in Europe). This left the Jewish people as the only group of any significant population that was allowed to loan money. This is what set the stage for a "Merchant Class."

Because they could loan money, and many other areas of activity were blocked to them, the Jews often became moneylenders. In addition, their religion and tight community had already set up a strong fabric of networking and connections and tradition. These elements combined to create a distinct group of traders and merchants who served a needed purpose in the greater community but also had its own traditions and customs.

The other significant custom or practice around money at this time was the practice of the Catholic Church of selling indulgences. What indulgences were is an odd concept in the 20$^{th}$ century, but was of paramount significance during the Middle

Ages. Essentially, an indulgence was a bribe for God. In exchange for donations of money (or land) the Church proclaimed that God would overlook the sins of the contributor without the need for penance or for reforming his ways. As one might imagine only the very wealthy could afford indulgences.

These customs around money and coins had the odd effect of tying pentacles and money closely to spirituality and belief systems. What you did with money was as much of an outward sign of your belief systems as it was a sign of your economic status. This also tied money into questions of justice as the Justice of God was a particularly popular point of thought and debate during the Middle Ages. The very people who had most access to coins were constantly involved in questions of justice. Churchmen and noblemen were by definition of their jobs asked to serve as both actual judges and models of the justice of the time.

Another aspect to coins or pentacles is that the people who actively used them were quite often travelers. Even nobles and the Church made extensive use of barter and trade. Land, chickens, services, and almost anything that was considered to be of value was traded and used for payment of most debts in the way we use money today. So, even though the Church and nobles had access to coinage, they did not often use it. Mostly it was used was when traveling in an area where the locals did not know you. If you were a stranger typically barter was a bit more difficult and certainly coins are easier to carry than either land or chickens. The merchant class of course did travel in order to arrange deals, get goods, and collect on loans. Thus, coins became part of the equipment one took on a journey if one could get them.

Then, as it is now, money was a symbol of status and offered a certain amount of security. It however brought with it other forms of experience and outlook. Those that traded in coins/pentacles were often obsessed with ideas of protection and spiritual belonging as well as with how to deal fairly or get away with dealing unfairly. In addition, coins brought with them a sense of being slightly outside the norm, and implied adventure and travel by their very existence.

For these reasons Pentacles are seen as symbols of success, abundance, travel, protection, and spiritual belief systems.

## Pentacles in Art and Literature

A good myth to really study to understand Pentacles better is Merchant of Venice. However, really look at the story. There are some wonderful explorations of what an agreement is, what constitutes true honor and what justice truly is in the play. These all have direct bearing on pentacles and are also elements of the play that are often overlooked at first.

To further explore Pentacles, you may also want to look at your own beliefs about money, right livelihood and abundance.

## Contemporary Customs and Traditions about Pentacles

Ever throw a penny in a fountain to make a wish? What about playing "heads or tails" by tossing a coin? These are examples of contemporary custom using the coin.

## Pentacles and the Element of Earth

Pentacles are associated with earth because the metal to make coins comes out of the earth. They are also associated with earth due to the fact that they can represent the seeds that a farmer uses to grow crops, which in turn get sold for coin (as well as represent an abundant crop come harvest time).

## Significance of Pentacles in a Reading

Questions to ask yourself when you encounter Pentacles in a reading include: What needs to be protected? Are my agreements and contracts with others fair? What do I have an abundance of and what do I do with that energy or object? What are my belief systems about money or work? How are my connections to various groups of people or communities in my life effecting how I go about my daily business?

## Expanding Your Personal Understanding of Pentacles

To further explore pentacles, you may also want to look at your own beliefs about money, right livelihood, and abundance. You may also want to read the Persephone and Demeter myth (Greek) or learn about the art and history of coin making.

## Expanding Your Personal Understanding of the Suits

I highly discourage you trying to memorize the following charts. However, looking them over and thinking about them can help your overall understanding of the suits, as well as assist you in creating your own personal definitions.

The first chart is a synthesis of the many meanings and qualities that Tarotists over the years have traditionally attributed to one suit or another. They are interesting to look at and provide one way to distill the information regarding the individual suits. If you are so inclined you can study them. You should be able to see from the discussion of the history and uses of each of the symbols where each of the correspondences has its origin.

If you are familiar with any of the myths listed, this should add extra meaning and body to your readings. If not, do not worry. Mythology is an important topic to study if you are serious about the Tarot, but remember that Tarot is a life long art and you have plenty of time.

**Chart of Traditional Correspondences for Minor Arcana Meanings**

|  | Swords | Wands | Cups | Pentacles |
|---|---|---|---|---|
| Elements | Air | Fire | Water | Earth |
| Occupations | Soldier, politician, scholar | Farmer, hunter, pilgrim | Clergy, doctor/ healer, midwife | Merchant, skilled, craftsman |
| Identity Focus | Heritage, "higher cause" | Community, custom, "sense of belonging" | Family, close friends, "love" | Self-reliance |
| Psychological Outlooks | Prejudice towards thinking independently | Prejudice towards personal experience | Prejudice towards intuition | Prejudice towards ability |
| Virtues | Courage, love of truth & justice | Insight, creativity, passion | Loyal, empathetic, forgiving | Responsible, persistent, creative |
| Vices | Judgmental, power seeking, callousness | Pride, impatience, unbending | Addictive, moody, overwhelmed | Judgmental, materialistic, stubborn |

## Mythological Associations for Suits of the Minor Arcana

| | Swords | Wands | Cups | Pentacles |
|---|---|---|---|---|
| Celtic (Irish, Welsh or Scottish) | Nuada's Sword: Assoc. with healing, smiths, magic & warfare also the Glaive of Light | Lugh's Spear: Protected against Balor's Evil Eye | Cerridwens Cauldron, "Dagadasor" also Dagda's Cauldron: | Lugh's Magic Stone: Known to deflect evil back to the Sender. |
| Grail Myths (French/Italian- 12th century) | Sword of Spirit: King David's Sword  Excalibur | Lance of Longinus: Pierced Christ's side | The Grail: The cup from the Last Supper Restores youth. | The stone platter used at the last supper |
| Greek Mythology | Sword of Fate: One of Nemesis' tools. | Apple Wand of Nemesis | Cup of Truth: Owned by Nemesis | Nemesis' Wheel: A symbol of wealth and craftsmanship |
| Teutonic Myth (Nordic) | Heimdal's Sword: "Guards the way to the spirit world".  Or Freya's Sword: "Cuts the air of its own accord". | Tyw's Spear: Symbol of Judicial Authority | Bowl of Sigyn: Used to catch poison and keep it away from her husband (he was chained beneath a poisonous snake) | Necklace which Freya received from the dwarves, symbol of bounty, craftsmanship and exchange |
| Hindu Myth | Sword of the God: Shiva's Trident | Ardhanari's Scepter of Authority | Cup of Ardhanari | Wheel of Fortune |

# Lesson Six
# Connecting Numbers with Suit Meanings

- ➤ The Numbers Have Meanings for Your Subconscious Mind
- ➤ Numbers in our Culture
- ➤ Numbers in Nature
- ➤ Common Themes in Numbered Cards
- ➤ Organizing and Recognizing What You Already Know About Numbers
- ➤ Getting to Know "Traditional" Meanings of Numbers
- ➤ Combining Numbers with Suit Meanings
- ➤ Review of Your Own Understanding of Suit Meanings
- ➤ Combining Observation, Suit Meanings, and Numerical Meanings
- ➤ Trusting Your Own Understanding of the Cards

# Getting to Know the Number Meanings of the Cards

In this book, we are examining the cards from four different perspectives in order to create for you a basic idea of what they mean and the wisdom they hold. We are looking at the cards in terms of the basic information that you can get from looking at a card without looking up a "meaning" in a book. The four areas of information we can get from looking at a card are:

1) Personal relationship (What do you see in the picture? What do you feel and notice when you look at the card?)

2) The structure of the deck (What kind of card is it? Minor Arcana or Major Arcana? If Minor, what suit? If Major, at what point on the Journey of The Fool is this card?)

3) Secondary symbolism (What are the tiny details in the card in terms of design, color and decoration, and what meanings do they suggest either intellectually or intuitively?)

4) Numerology

In a way, Numerology is what ties it all together. It helps us remember that while each card is an independent messenger, it is also part of a larger deck. The numbers help us connect back to the overall structure of the deck and understand where the card we are looking at fits in terms of the big picture. The numbers help us to know what other cards in a reading (or missing from a reading) might have messages particularly connected to each other, and gives us a sense of "where on the journey" we or the people we are reading for might be. For example, if you found in a reading that you had three suit cards numbered ten but not the fourth, this might bring up some interesting questions for you as a reader. Why is the last ten missing, is there a message there? At the same point, the fact that three of the ten cards did appear is also of importance. Also, if you have lots of numbered cards that are low numbers (1s and 2s etc.) you might add to your reading an understanding that things are just starting off or getting started.

Of course, this is only one such way to use the numbers on the cards. There is a whole study of Numerology that one can utilize into the Tarot that goes much deeper than this aspect. Fortunately for you, you already probably have a deeper sense of Numerology than you think.

## The Numbers Have Meanings for Your Subconscious Mind

It may seem odd at first to think of numbers as something that give you information without you having to look it up in a book, but they do. Just as you discovered when you were learning about the different suits that you already have conscious or subconscious associations with the stories and myths that lend the different suits their meanings, you already have associations with the meanings of numbers.

From our experiences with our bodies and with nature (we have two eyes, but five senses etc.), we learn about numbers. In addition, we also have plenty of games, poems, songs, and traditions about numbers in both folk and popular culture (the song lyrics "one is the loneliest number" and "tea for two" for example.) The meanings of numbers literally surround us. We simply have to notice.

## Exercise 6A: Numbers in our Culture

Take a few minutes and simply write down every example you can think of about what numbers mean from songs, stories, superstitions, children's games, movies and other cultural influences that relate to numbers, particularly to the numbers 1-10. (For example: good sprits grant three wishes, or the seventh son of the seventh son is supposed to be psychic.) Don't worry about right or wrong, or if you agree or disagree with these interpretations. For now, we are simply finding out the associations with number meanings that are already in your subconscious mind.

If you get stuck think about:
- Which numbers are associated with good/bad luck?
- Customs for special days like weddings and birthdays
- Children's counting games
- Folktales and fairytales

_____
_____
_____
_____
_____
_____
_____
_____
_____
_____
_____
_____
_____
_____
_____
_____
_____

## Exercise 6B: Numbers in Nature

Now, take another few minutes and think about numbers in terms of nature. For example, you might think of four seasons, two hands, five senses etc. Again, don't worry about a right or wrong answer, simply brainstorm and see what comes to mind.

Be sure to think about:
- Plants, seeds, fruits, leaves, and flowers
- Animals
- Planets and celestial bodies
- Seasons (remember farther away or closer to the equator the seasons change)
- Insects and birds

_____
_____
_____
_____
_____
_____
_____
_____
_____
_____
_____
_____
_____
_____
_____

## Exercise 6C: Common Themes

This exercise should take you about an hour, about five or six minutes for each number. All you need to do is pull out of your deck the four Minor Arcana cards of each number, do not include the Court Cards (characters of the Minor Arcana) and spend about five minutes noticing what themes seem to be common to all four cards, what themes seem to be different, and any other thoughts that strike you. Then as we have done before when just starting to explore particular aspects of a card, create a meaning for that number based on what you are actually seeing and observing in the cards. Write your observations in the space provided.

_____
_____
_____
_____
_____
_____
_____

## Example: Meaning of the Number Six through Intuition and Observation

All of the sixes seem very active. In the Swords and Wands card there is travel (a man poling a boat across a river, with two cloaked figures in it, a youth on a horse in a celebration of some sort) and in the pentacles and cups cards there seems to be an action of giving going on (a boy giving a little girl flowers, a man giving two kneeling people coins). The cups and wands card seem to depict very happy scenes, but the pentacles and swords seem to me to be fairly happy too, but more like relief happy, as if times have been tough but are now getting better through the aid of others. So, if I had to make up a common meaning that might capture what I am seeing and feeling from all four cards I might say "A balance of giving and receiving, a time of reaping what we have sowed".

# Key Words and Meanings for Numbers One through Ten, as Associated with Tarot

| Quality | Ones | Twos | Threes | Fours | Fives |
|---|---|---|---|---|---|
| Leadership Skills | Focus | Balance | Compassion | Organization | Discernment |
| Creative Focus | Beginning | Growth/ Movement | Expansion | Stabilization | Modification |
| Stage of Growth | Initial Inspiration | Conception | Gestation | Formation | Realization |
| Spiritual Gift* | Highest Potential | Wisdom | Understanding | Mercy/ Support | Judgment/ Power |
| Learning Approach | Revelation | Communion | Exploration | Imitation | Critique |

| Quality | Sixes | Sevens | Eights | Nines | Tens |
|---|---|---|---|---|---|
| Leadership Skills | Gratitude | Introspection | Intellect | Intuition | Action |
| Creative Focus | Renewal | Integration | Evaluation | Imagination | Manifestation |
| Stage of Growth | Appreciation | Separation | Observation | Acceptance | Receiving |
| Spiritual Gift* | Harmony | Victory | Glory | Foundation | Kingdom |
| Learning Approach | Synthesis | Contemplation | Analysis | Creativity | Experience |

*The spiritual gift aspect of this chart is taken from associating the numbers of the Tarot with key points on the Kabalistic Tree of Life (Sephiroth). Like Astrology, Qaballah (Kaballah) is an independent discipline that many Tarotists study in addition to studying the Tarot as the two spiritual disciplines have many associations and connections.

## Exercise 6D: Getting to Know "Traditional" Meanings for the Numbers

Take some time to study the chart you have just completed. When you look at the chart are there areas of it that immediately make sense to you? On the other hand, are there certain areas that immediately confuse you? How does it compare to your own chart of number meanings?

Ask yourself why certain words and key concepts are associated with certain numbers.

## Combining Numerical Meanings with Suit Meanings

Once we have a strong sense of the numbers, we need to match our understanding of the numbers with our understanding of the individual suits. After all, in a Tarot reading you are looking at specific cards such as the Seven of Swords or the Ten of Wands instead of just looking abstractly at the number 7 or the number 10. In order to do that we need to start by making sure that your knowledge of the four suits is fully integrated and easy for you to remember and use.

## Exercise 6E: Review Your Own Meanings

This is a review of what we have been covering in the last few lessons. Although it is a review, you will find that your progress in the next few lessons goes much more smoothly if you take the time to do this exercise. The Tarot is a tool that is designed to adapt to our subconscious minds. Whatever is in your deep mind is not what is in anyone else's deep mind. The Tarot is flexible enough to handle that fact.

Imagine you are holding a Sword (if you actually have a sword get it and hold it or keep it near you so you can focus on it.)

- What thoughts come to mind?
- What do you want to do?
- What do you feel? What do experiences from your life does holding this sword makes you remember?
- What natural element does the sword make you think about?
- How does this element behave in nature, and how does it affect things around it?

Taking all these impressions into consideration, answer the following: What do Swords mean to you?

_____
_____
_____
_____
_____
_____
_____
_____
_____

What do Wands mean to you?

_____
_____
_____
_____
_____
_____
_____

What do Cups mean to you?
_____
_____
_____
_____
_____
_____
_____

What do Pentacles mean to you?
_____
_____
_____
_____
_____
_____
_____

## Example of Reviewing Your Own Meanings for Cups

When I imagine holding a cup, I see this cup as my mortar and pestle, and I am blending an herbal remedy for one of my clients. Other times, I see myself slowly sipping and savoring a cup of hot green tea.

I feel open; intuitively knowing what is needed in the moment. I know that this cup before me will never be empty, as this vessel contains the Universal energies, and it is brimming with all that there is. For me personally Cups represent relationships, emotions, and intuition.

## Combined Suit and Number Meaning for the Six of Cups

***Personal Number Meaning:*** A balance of giving and receiving, a time of taking things in and knowing just what the right outward action is. Possibly renewal or some sort of acceptance of life's "turns and cycles."

***Traditional Number Meanings:*** Gratitude, Renewal, Appreciation, Harmony, Synthesis

***Suit meaning:*** Relationships, emotions, community and the capacity for both obsession and change, especially in relationships.

***Combined Meaning:*** A renewal in relationships is possible through a balance of giving and receiving. It is time to accept that a relationship is changing and that it is probably good change.

## Exercise 6F: Combining Observation, Suit Meanings and Number Meanings to Finalize Your Personal Meaning for a Minor Arcana Card

The next step of this exercise is to take the meaning you now have in mind, and look once again at the card. See if the picture itself suggests any additional information or insight. Then combine your intuitive observations of the card with what you have learned about it by looking at the suit and the number. A meaning you know is right for you and will work for you. What is your meaning?

_____
_____
_____
_____

## Final Meaning of the 6 of Cups

When I look at the picture I am struck by the bright sunny colors, the youth and innocence of the children and the flowers that seem to be lilies (remind me of funerals) and roses (remind me of romance.)

The meanings I take from these symbols are to go ahead and let things die that need to die, (lilies) and to also lighten up and have more fun (bright colors, children) and trust the gifts that are on the way.

My meaning for the card based on the suit and number is: A renewal in relationships is possible through a balance of giving and receiving. It is time to accept that a relationship is changing and that it is probably a good change.

## Trusting Your Own Understanding of the Cards

Above, you have an example of a card meaning I came up with for the Six of Cups. It is a personal meaning that came out of my own relationship to the picture on the card, the suit the card belongs to, and the number on the card. But should I trust it? After all, aren't there Tarot experts who have come up with what the card "should" mean? The answer is that it is usually better to understand how the experts came to their conclusions than it is to simply follow them blindly, or rebel and ignore them altogether.

It is our goal in this class to help you fully learn the Tarot and deeply integrate your own understanding of what the cards mean to you. This is different from the approach of simply memorizing a bunch of meanings without really knowing what they are based on, which will lead to a shallow relationship with the Tarot, and make it hard for you to answer complex or emotionally charged questions in a reading.

It is also different from looking at the cards and only making up a meaning on the spur of the moment based on your personal reactions. Reacting too spontaneously will leave you with an understanding of the cards that might be unpredictable and get you confused in readings. It will also tend to make it harder for you to discover and integrate some of the deeper spiritual lessons that are hidden in the Tarot.

I have also found that if your interpretations are too changeable, your clients will wonder why the same cards have different meanings and begin to question your interpretative abilities. Instead, we are consciously and deliberately going back and forth between both approaches until you come to a third way of relating to the cards, which is to develop a personal understanding of what the cards mean that you can back up both emotionally and intellectually because it is based on a firm foundation of both theory and personal experience.

This is what we have done in our example by combining personal impressions of the symbols with information gathered from studying the numbers and the suits. We are combining traditional understanding with personal understanding to form deeper insight. How well does this approach work? Well, you will have to judge for yourself, but here is an example that might help you to see the power of taking the time to really discover your own meanings for the cards and then sticking with those meanings. So, when finding some authority's definition of a card, ask yourself the following:

1) Will I really remember this meaning? Does it ring true to me?

2) When I say this interpretation to a client, will it sound like my own definition? Or will it sound like a rehearsed answer?

3) What insight do I get from that definition?

4) Is it flexible enough to work for the numerous positions of a spread it can appear in and the myriad of questions that can be posed?

In almost all cases you will find that your own meanings are easier to remember and will make more sense to you in terms of specific advice if they are your own meanings. Use the work of experts to push your own understanding deeper and farther, not to replace it.

# Lesson Seven: The Court Cards

- What are Court Cards?
- The Function of a Court
- The Different Jobs of the Court
- Court Cards can be seen as Aspects of Self
- Exercise 7A: Court Cards within Us
- Exercise 7B: Understanding more about Court Cards as Aspects of Self
- Court Cards as Key Players in our lives
- Exercise 7C: Court Cards in the World around us
- Exercise 7D: Advanced Work in Understanding Court Cards
- Traditional Meanings of Court Cards

## What are the Court Cards?

The Court Cards are some of the most magical and also most difficult to interpret cards in the deck. This is because they have powers often overlooked by those new to reading Tarot. They are here to teach us a great deal about ourselves by teaching us about three key elements that shape our identity:

1) The roles we take on in the world around us,

2) The people who influence us most,

3) Our core attitudes or way of approaching the world (skills and personality).

Unfortunately, Court Cards are rarely explained to the seeker of Tarot in this way. Usually their meanings are either glossed over or the information is there but the theory to understand that information is not supplied.

Everyone is familiar with the old stereotype of the fortuneteller saying, "you will meet a dark and handsome man." Most Tarotists scoff at this as both too predictive and too shallow to be real Tarot. And yet, many Tarot books will essentially describe the Court Cards in exactly this way.

For example, in The Pictorial Key to the Tarot, the author, A.E. Waite, describes the Queen of Cups in this way:

> "A dark woman, countrywoman, friendly, chaste, loving, honorable."

Given these kinds of explanations of the cards, how else is a reader supposed to interpret the Tarot Courts? The answer is by understanding that Court Cards are here to ask us complex questions that encourage us to bridge our practical knowledge with spiritual understanding, and are more than here to supply simple meanings about what has happened or will happen. If the other cards answer "the what", then the Court Cards are "the who". The key is that when "the who" changes, often the entire meaning of the reading also changes.

Think of it this way. Imagine that as you find yourself reading you encounter one Minor Arcana card with the essential meaning of "get off your behind and take some practical action about your money situation" and a Major Arcana card in the same reading with the essential message of "go deep within yourself, find your center, and your true success will come from taking risks and accepting change." The messages still need to be put into action and applied by the client into his or her life. If the person is a naive and exuberant adolescent with little life experience then those messages might lead to a completely different set of insights and actions than if the person is a somewhat seasoned and cynical old business man.

The Court Cards in a reading are there to help us understand ourselves and others more fully so that we can put to better use all the other insight and instruction the Tarot has to give us. In order to unlock that understanding we need to first know what a Court is and does. By knowing why these cards were named Court Cards and shaped after the roles of individuals in a Court, we get a glimpse into the kinds of things these cards are asking us to learn about ourselves and the people around us.

## The Function of a Court

It is hard for modern people to understand Court Cards because many people do not know what a Court truly is. Simply speaking a Court (in the Royal sense) is a group of people who have been charged with the administration and ruling of a land or a group of citizens while at the same time providing inspiration and entertainment to the masses. It is rather like combining the U.S. institutions of Capitol Hill and Hollywood into one if you can imagine such a thing! Those of you who may have seen the movie "The Knight's Tale", based on one of Chaucer's CANTERBURY TALES have a good idea what is meant by this.

The primary function of the Court was the efficient ruling of the land. Simply speaking, a good Court should do what any good government does: serve the people as a whole. And, like governments everywhere, Courts have not always done the job properly. The Tarot was formed on the ideals of what a good

Court (or government) should do, and not on what they actually do.

The Court's secondary objective was serving as entertainment, something that might be hard for us to grasp in this day and age. It is easy to forget, but at the time that Tarot was really taking root, there was no TV, movies, Internet, or radio, or even printed books. News and entertainment was much harder to come across than we can even imagine. The Court was charged with the role of being an antidote to this situation. After all, happy people rarely challenge authority, so entertaining the masses helped them protect their position.

The members of the Court had the unique ability to bring into daily life excitement and adventure. For one thing Knights and Pages traveled a great deal more than the average person, and so could share news of the places they had been and tales of the glorious battles they had seen or in which they had taken part.

The Court provided glamour. The only fine clothing and beautiful luxuries to be had would go first to the King and Queen and then to the other nobles. So, in the way that modern people are fascinated with "Lifestyles of the Rich and Famous," people of this time period were fascinated with ballads and stories of the doings of the Court.

This put the members of the Court in a dilemma. On the one had they were supposed to rule efficiently and effectively at the job of being at Court, whereas on the other hand they were to provide a template on which the people as a whole could project their fears and fantasies and political and personal agendas. (Again, rather like we still do with our public officials.)

One way to understand the role of a Court that is closer to "home" for most people is to look at what is needed to run a small business or a household efficiently. After all, we have all had times in our lives where our home and family situation has run smoothly and times when it has not. We have also all had times when we worked for, or were somehow affected by, a business that did not run smoothly. The consequences of such experiences make us all experts on some of the aspects of ruling and organizing. After all, you know better than anybody else what it is like when your bills do not get paid on time or your laundry is left undone and what steps are best taken to make sure such occurrences are as rare as possible. You also know of a thousand things that would make your loved one's lives run smoother or your favorite business' procedures more effective and efficient if they would only listen to you. When you are looking at the world from that particular perspective you are looking at the world from a Court perspective. From farmers to janitors to lawmakers to movie stars we all have the inherent qualities of King and Queen, Knight and Page. It is just that we tend to not think of our talents in that way.

One of the biggest duties required of a Court is the ability to make and uphold laws. While few of us find ourselves writing legislation, passing decrees, or even setting policies for major businesses, all of us find ourselves making laws in the course of our normal lives. Should you set your teenager's curfew at 10:00 or 12:00? That is a decision of law.

## Different Jobs of the Court

### *Role of Kings*

Although there is a long tradition of the "divine right of Kings" and they have been a political staple throughout most of human politics, the role did not simply spring into being. The roles and responsibilities of Kingship have been developed and defined over time according to the needs of the societies that have created Kings.

Many tribal and indigenous peoples do not have Kings. They tend to have elders, councils of leaders, or even chiefs, but not Kings as we understand the term. The need for Kingship seems to come into play with the rise of militarism and the need to band together several different tribes or clans under a single military strategy under one ruler.

According to the spiritual and historical researcher Starhawk, the role of King, at least in Mesopotamia and the Middle East, was originally a temporary position granted to the consort of the female political leader during times of war. However, the idea evolved. It is certain that everywhere there have been Kings there has been a clear indication that it was the King's job above all else to protect the people in times of war and specifically to protect and ensure the fertility of the land (often through the protection of a Queen as a living symbol of such fertility). This is in fact the basis of the entire feudal system that was the political system and social fabric within which the Tarot took hold.

Early on, any rich man with land might end up as a King if he could convince all the Lords that he was the best military leader, and in fact many civil wars have been waged throughout the world by claimants to the throne who may have had only a slight amount of royal blood, but who possessed a great amount of military and political savvy. The primary role of any King is therefore political and military protection.

Such a tremendous job and one of such importance quickly led to a need to imbue the King with certain mystical qualities. Early on, Kings were seen as the Talismans of good fortune for their people and were said to be "married to the land." This tradition which has its roots in the King being chosen by the female leader of the tribe placed the King in a mystical union with the land and made him a living embodiment of the vitality and fertility of his land. This eventually led to the concept of the divine right of Kings and the idea that the King represented the word of God on Earth. The Church took the place that was once the matriarchs and anointed the Kings appointing them with sacred authority and responsibility.

As such, the King's secondary responsibility was the increase of his abundance and fertility. In Medieval times, this was interpreted to mean securing the spiritual well- being of the land, securing a suitable heir to the throne, and developing a sound and flourishing economy. Obviously not all Kings have been able to meet all of these requirements, but nonetheless the job of the King has remained essentially the same.

Kings therefore represent: Protection, Long Range Planning, Strategy, Politics, Law, Justice, and Contractual Agreements.

You are using King qualities in your own life when: You make major purchasing decisions, engage in any legal battles or activities, chart your career path, or set firm rules for yourself or your household.

## *The Role of Queens*

The role of Queens is arguably somewhat older than the role of Kings. There is sufficient archeological evidence to suggest that in many areas around the world, the early rulers were female. Whereas the authority granted to the role of King seems to have come from the need for protection, the authority granted to the female matriarch whose role became that of Queen seems to have come from reverence for fertility. As the bearers of children, and the ones primarily responsible with the gathering of plant forms of nutrition, women became associated with the "Mother Earth" and with nurturing, fertility, and comfort. The role of the Queen has remained strongly tied to these principals.

The Queen more than any other member of the Court became the living symbol of the ideas of the land and its psychological and spiritual keeper. While the Church vied very strongly for this role, again and again in country after country it became the Queen or her representative who actually took on this role. Much of this was due to the fact that rural people to this day identify with a Mother Earth or a Lady of the Grains and the Queen represented that role in ceremony, art, and the hearts of many subjects. It is, after all, easier to picture a lovely Queen as the spiritual embodiment of a land than it is to picture a whole host of church officials in their robes.

This is particularly true at the time when Tarot was gaining popularity. During the height of the "romance" or epic tale of Knights and their Lady's, the Queen or Lady who embodied virtue was an absolute essential to all of these stories. These were far more than just fairy tales. They represented the values of an entire culture and communicated those values to the next generation. They were an expression of exactly what the people wanted their Queens to be. The role was laid out and expressed quite clearly.

The Queen was supposed to embody the qualities of fertility, spiritual purity, and mercy. She was deemed the representative of the Holy Virgin or the Mother Goddess on earth and was supposed to inspire her King and her people to proper action through her simple presence. While it was the King's job to protect and plan for these things, it was the Queen's job to be them. The King was married to the land, and the Queen was the land. As a living representative of the land it was the Queen's job to make sure that the values of the society, particularly the more spiritual values, were being nurtured and tended to with care.

For the actual woman who took on the role this meant many things. The Queen was supposed to excel at ceremonial and ritual occasions. She was also supposed to tend to all domestic business and make sure that the internal affairs of the country were handled efficiently and correctly. The Queen thus became responsible for what we would think of now as social policy. Where the King might make laws and prepare for war, the Queen might champion the cause of a falsely accused man or ensure that there was a place to tend to wounded warriors. She would also see that the marriages, funerals, education, and other turning points of her subjects were correctly attended to and provided for. Above all however it was the job of the Queen to bear and raise the next King and thus ensure the ongoing fertility and protection of the land.

Queens therefore represent: Inspiration, Fertility, Creativity, Charity, Social Justice, and Ceremony. You are using Queen qualities in your own life when: You volunteer for local charities, attend social occasions to please or impress others, serve as a role model, create art, care for children, fight injustice, and encourage manners or spiritual values.

## *The Role of Knights*

The role of the Knight is to roam the countryside and get things done. As the only member of the Court that both has easy access to transportation (horses) and is not tied by his job to a specific spot like the King and Queen are, the Knight is the "field representative" of the Court. The Knight's role is to uphold honor and to get specific things done at the discretion of the King. They don't wage war as a King does, they make sure that they secure the river from invaders, or escort the Queen to safety or any of the thousand specific actions that make the society they live in work. Knights therefore represent: Strength, competition, honor, action, and administration.

You are using Knight qualities in your own life when: You spend a day rushing around catching up on errands and personal business, engage in competition, challenge someone who you feel is acting unethically, and carry out specific tasks that are crucial to a larger plan.

## *The Role of Pages*

Pages were typically Knights in training and servants to the Court. They held a higher place than normal servants, but were still there primarily to serve others at Court. Often, they were also political hostages. They were frequently the younger sons from the families of the King's rivals, there under the polite guise of being trained at battle and in the ways of the Court. Essentially, they were there however to ensure that their relatives did not try to attack the King, and if they did, then the Page would lose his life. Pages were very frequently pawns in political games and spies for various families of the Court. They are the only members of the Court that were not expected to take a role in public ceremony or as a public symbol. Instead they were meant to be learning everything they needed to know in order to take on these roles in the future. The combination of clerical duties and political intrigue created a precarious position for the Page and left the Page having to keep track of everything. Information was the key power and survival skill for a Page as fetching, carrying, and delivering messages that must all be memorized word for word was their foremost responsibility.

Pages can represent: Education, memorization, messages, communication, information, duty and preparation for the future.

You are using Page qualities in your own life when: You observe a situation from behind the scenes, send or receive messages, study, learn a new skill, perform helpful tasks for someone you love or respect, or attempt to mediate tense or uncomfortable situations.

## Court Cards Can Be Seen as Aspects of Self

Court Cards represent questions of attitude & self-identity in readings. One of the major secrets of the Tarot is that we are at one time or another every card in the deck. We have inside of us each card and we use (and sometimes misuse) each card's qualities and lessons in different aspects of our lives. Different Court Cards can represent among other things:

- ✓ How we solve problems
- ✓ What we view as worthwhile
- ✓ What we avoid
- ✓ What we desire
- ✓ What we are most likely to notice in others
- ✓ Our "public face" or how we strive to have others see us
- ✓ What we are like to be around when at rest and at ease
- ✓ What we are like to be around under times of stress and strain

## Exercise 7A: Court Cards within Us

1) Pull out all of the Pages from your deck. Without going back over the information in this section what do you remember about the role that a Page plays at court?

_____
_____
_____
_____
_____
_____
_____

2) What stands out in your memory about what Pages do based on both these class notes and on any other associations you might have with Pages from reading about history, seeing movies, from books you have read, or stories you have been told?

_____
_____
_____
_____
_____
_____
_____
_____
_____

3) Think of fictional characters and real people you know. Who seems like a Page?

_____
_____
_____
_____
_____
_____
_____
_____
_____
_____
_____
_____
_____

4) Based on that, what types of attitudes and skills do you think a person needs to be a good Page?

_____
_____
_____
_____

5) Now look at the details in all four cards in front of you. What similarities and differences do you notice? Take the time to really study the background details before recording your response.

_____
_____
_____
_____
_____
_____
_____
_____

6) Simply state for yourself and in your own words what Pages mean to you.

_____
_____
_____
_____
_____
_____
_____

7) How comfortable are you with the Page aspect of yourself? In which area of life (suit) are you most like a Page? In which area of life are you least like a Page?

_____
_____
_____
_____
_____
_____
_____
_____
_____

Repeat the exercise with each of the remaining Court Cards and record in your journal for future reference.

## Example: Court Cards within Us: Pages

I remember that Pages are essentially messengers. Usually they got sent to Court very young, and had to learn how to keep up with the intrigue very quickly in order to survive.

I think modern day Pages are young people with their first jobs, those new to the corporate ladder of business, those who are students, and especially those who are in apprenticeships for a trade or family business. I think of my former assistant, who was expected to work during the day to learn my trade hands on, and study at night and during slower times to learn the textbook know-how of my industry.

To excel in either situation I think a person needs to be curious, intelligent, and a keen observer with the energy and motivation to succeed.

When I look at all the Pages together I notice that they are all outside and alone, and that all of them seem to be studying their objects very carefully. They all have hats except the Page of Swords, likely because of his/her air/intellectual aspects. Since the hat would cover the crown, its possible the Page of Swords would find it as a hindrance to accessing this energy. The Page of Cups has what appears to be a live fish in his/her cup which is the only "companion" any of the Pages seem to have to represent her connection with emotion and intuition. The Page of Wands is the only one with a traveling cloak to represent her energy.

I think Pages mean learning and figuring out how to use your own tools and find your own way, often in a complex world. I also think they are about sorting out what information is useful and what is not.

## Exercise 7B: Understanding More about Court Cards as Aspects of Self

Another very illuminating exercise is to separate out all the Court (you should have 16 cards) then shuffle and draw a card for each of the points listed in the section above entitled 'Court Cards Can Be Seen As Aspects of Self'. Assume the Card represents an accurate depiction of that aspect of your self and really examine and intuit on the card. Record your results in your journal.

## Court Cards can be seen as Key Players in Our Lives

In addition to helping us understand the obvious roles we take on and the qualities we express in life, the Court Cards can help us to understand some of the more subtle patterns in relationships we might be creating as well.

What we believe will affect our actions and cause us to attract certain people/situations into our lives and keep certain people/situations away from us. This is called the law of attraction, of like attracting like. One of the things the Court Cards do for us in a reading is the act of mirroring. Simply put, this is a metaphysical truth states that if I have an aspect of my personality, for example, impatience, that is particularly strong, I will draw people with that same aspect into my life. Thus, I will be surrounded by impatient people. This will happen until it is so obvious that I am surrounded by impatient people that I will have no choice but to confront the situation. The good news is that this gives me an opportunity to see in others what is strongly present in myself, in order to help me learn more about it.

To go back to the idea of the fortuneteller uttering predictions about tall dark strangers, the idea here is to ask ourselves why do we keep running into so many tall dark strangers when what we really want a short blonde friend. When they show up in a reading they often indicate both someone who is affecting our situation and an aspect of how we are or could respond to the situation at hand.

## Exercise 7C: Court Cards in the World Around Us
*(Learning from the Key Players in Our Lives)*

Choose a single Court Card for this exercise. Remember to set sacred space and prepare to do intuitive work just as you did in lesson one. Do not skip any steps. Examine the card and answer the following questions:

What do you think of when you consider the job of this Court Card? In addition to the descriptions in this lesson, think back on movies, novels, history class, and anything else that has left you with a sense (accurate or otherwise) of the "job" this type of person (Court Type) has.
Who specifically in your life reminds you of this type of Court Card? Write down their name and the specific attitudes, skills and qualities that these individuals bring to mind.

_____
_____
_____
_____
_____
_____
_____
_____
_____

What do they have or know that you don't? What do you have or know that they don't?

_____
_____
_____
_____
_____
_____
_____
_____
_____
_____

Remembering what the suit for this card means, how do the images and ideas you have about this court type apply to the suit in question?

Based on your above answers and your own imagination, what do you think the essential qualities and lessons this type of person represents?

_____
_____
_____
_____
_____
_____
_____
_____
_____
_____

What do I have to learn from this type of person in order to be the best possible me I can be and make the most of the opportunities around me?

_____
_____
_____
_____
_____
_____
_____
_____

## Example: Court Cards in the World Around Us

### *Queen of Wands*

When I think of the Queen of Wands I think of her having to "hold a kingdom together" and of having to produce and heir. I also think of nurturing what is good about a country. For example, Elizabeth was a patron of the arts and particularly a patron to Shakespeare. Also, for me the Queen is the epitome of womanhood in general, so for me it means achieving the highest aspects of the Feminine Self as portrayed by the particular suit she represents. In this case, the Queen of Wands, being the most active of the Queens, represents her passion, determination, and energy to get the job done.

I am able to see how I am the Queen. In my work, I have to coach and nurture others, but at the same time I have to be grounded and "tell it like it is" to get them to be responsible for their own health and happiness. I also am a wellness coach and specialty foods chef and author, so I need to wear many hats, whereas the proprietor serves as the one responsible for customer relations, taxes, and other responsibilities. Queens are strategists. I am always planning on what to do next week, the next workshop, the next product line, and therefore I do not waste time on the "little things." I am definitely the mother to the staff, and am the one who creates the atmosphere, the aura, the substance of the store without being in total charge of it. I make shopping here the experience that it is.

> Remember what the suit for this card means. How do the images and ideas you have about this court type apply to the suit in question?

_____
_____
_____
_____
_____
_____
_____
_____
_____
_____

# Exercise 7D: Understanding Court Cards as Personal Mirrors

1) What roles do you let others play or expect others to play in your life?

2) If you had to assign a different Court Card to each of the 16 most influential people in your life, which Cards would you assign to which people?

3) Each night for 16 nights choose a person first and write about a paragraph about how they effect your life and what you think about them in general. Then pick a Court Card that they remind you of, or that seems to represent what you think about them. Then carefully examine the card being sure to write down what you notice about both the primary and secondary symbolism in the card and your overall interpretation of the card. Do this portion of your work in your journal.

4) At the end of the 16 nights go back and read your paragraphs, and assume that they are not really about the other people but they are about aspects of yourself instead. What do you particularly like? What do you not like? Does reading these paragraphs as though they were about you make you want to make any changes? And what does that teach you about yourself?

_____
_____
_____
_____
_____
_____
_____
_____
_____
_____
_____
_____
_____

5) At the end of this exercise write down 3 positive things you have learned or committed to learning and set aside the rest of your 16 meanings. For the next month or so notice when the Court Cards that you most associate with your 3 positive leanings show up in readings. What other secrets and encouragement do they have for you?

_____

_____

_____

_____

_____

_____

_____

## Traditional Meanings of Court Cards

Now that you have discovered some of your own meanings for the Court Cards, take a look at some traditional meanings for them. Pick a standard meaning for a Court Card from a book or other Tarot source, and combine it with a standard suit meaning. Merge the two sentences into a single one to form a standard meaning for a specific Court Card. For example, you might choose Knights. The chart says that Knights ask us "What actions need to be taken?" and then you might choose Swords and they can mean: defense, strategy and information. Combining the two you come to a fairly standard interpretation of the Knight of Swords meaning strong actions to defend that which is precious, particularly through strategy and focusing on ideals.

Try this process of combining insights from the various "traditional meanings" sections in this lesson and see what you come up with for card meanings. What do you notice? Do you agree or disagree? How would you add to or alter the set meaning for this particular card? Once again it is not about being "right" but about understanding how you come to your own conclusions regarding card interpretation.

# Lesson Eight
# Understanding Reversed Cards

- The Challenge of Reversed Cards
- Historical Perspective on Reversed Cards
- Contemporary Perspectives on Reversed Cards
- Environmental Factors and Reversals
- Psychological Factors and Reversals
- Distinguishing Between Environmental and Psychological Interpretations
- Exercise 8A- Interpreting Reversed Cards

# The Challenge of Reversed Cards

Using reversed cards is perhaps the most challenging issue for students. There are a number of books out there, even decks, that do not utilize them, yet the use of reversed cards is core to properly reading the Tarot. After all, if every card has a myriad of symbols, then isn't there importance to the fact that the card was drawn upside down? So, what is a reader to do?

Learning how to interpret reversed cards is very rewarding, as it completes the Tarot story. Once you are comfortable working with reversed cards you will often find that the key to making a full reading or spread make sense lies in which cards are reversed and why. It is therefore very important to learn the use of reversed cards and how to make the most of them when they appear in a reading. While everything being covered here applies to the major Arcana as well, Chapter 13 will cover additional information on the importance of reversed Major Arcana, and their unique role in a reading.

There seems to be two key reasons that students have trouble with reversed cards. The first is that instead of actually examining what the card looks like upside down, students look for some generic and simple rule to follow, such as "reversed cards always mean the opposite of what they meant right side up". This is rarely accurate, and even when it holds some thread of truth, is it rarely as helpful as a long look at and intuitive interpretation of the card as it appears when it is reversed.

The second reason why people have difficulty with reversed cards is that many believe that a reversed card is solely about the negative. Reversed cards, like upright cards, can indicate unfavorable influences, but they are much more than just negative versions of the upright meanings. Reversed cards are used to indicate a rather abstract concept- and a concept on which our culture has greatly altered our interpretation over since the Tarot first came into popular use. Sometimes they have entirely different meanings altogether. Simply put, reversed cards are used to mark where a psychic or psychological impulse is present, but for one reason or another is not fully active. The process and reason for the impulses remaining inactive are understood in modern times in terms of psychology and New Age spirituality. In the Middle Ages, the processes and reasons for suppressing psychic and psychological energies where seen almost solely in terms of the conflict between God and the Devil, Good and Evil.

In order to delve into the differing worldviews regarding this suppression of energy, we first need a clear idea of what it means to experience a "psychic or psychological impulse which is not fully active." This sounds very academic and not very specific, but when you think about it, you have a hundred impulses a day that you do not act on. For example, I may wish to scream at a rude customer but choose not to do so; so, this is a "non-active energy," as the impulse is still there, and the feelings that surround it are still there, but the action expressing those feelings is not there. Instead, I block the energy inside me and do not let it out. This is an example of a "reversed" energy which I am consciously aware is there.

There are some types of reversed energies, however, of which we are not consciously aware. Take for example the impulse to bear children. Many women describe that as they become older this impulse suddenly surges forward and they begin to feel that their biological clock is ticking. Now in reality the biological clock these women speak of has been ticking since puberty, and the body prepares to bear a child monthly. It is simply a matter of timing. As the appropriate time to have a child approaches, and as the window of opportunity to have one appears to be closing, a biological desire, which has been there all along, comes forward in a stronger, harder to ignore manner. Another example of energy being suppressed without our conscious knowledge can come when we prepare to make painful decisions. Often people who decide to leave a marriage or move to a far away place will realize once they have made the decision that they were acting in ways that indicated their decision long before they personally even recognized that there was a problem. There are of course thousands of ways to experience reversed energy, either consciously or unconsciously. These examples are simply designed to help you recognize that such energies exist.

# Historical Perspective on Reversed Cards

Taking a look at how our societies have understood reversed energies and what we have chosen to do about them in various stages of history should help you to develop a deeper understanding of it.

To the Medieval mind, reversed energies were closely aligned with sin. There was no real distinction made between a psychic or spiritual impulse and a psychological one, and all realms of the human psyche were neatly divided into good and bad. It was the absolute duty of man to suppress a natural desire for bad in order to make room for God and good. It was believed that humanity (and especially the female population) was more prone towards sin than Godliness. Therefore, reversed energies most often meant the suppression of "evil impulses" within the soul. It was further believed that even a man who could successfully subdue the evil impulses within himself might very well encounter evil influences outside of himself which were trying to sway him from the path of righteousness or possibly take possession of his soul. Under this model there was absolutely no such thing as suppressing a good impulse or energy. If such an impulse was suppressed it was simply a matter of that energy being overpowered by a negative influence, which must be discovered and conquered. For example, in that world a proper woman did not wait to have a child but rightly and virtuously had one as soon as physically able. If for any reason she did not, an evil force was at play that needed to be found and counteracted.

Now, it may seem that I am over simplifying matters, but remember the Church was the primary political power in Medieval Europe and the conflict between God and the Devil was interpreted by the Church fathers very literally. While individuals may not have agreed with the above way of thinking, the culture as a whole acknowledged this worldview as "just the way things are." There is considerable artistic and internal evidence in the symbolism to assert that the Tarot was designed and used primarily by rebels whose ideas differed from the official Church rulings of the day. Nonetheless these ideas permeated the culture and there is no way that Tarot interpretation and tradition could have escaped this cultural influence.

According to the most prevalent thinking at the time, reversed cards indicated instances where a person was "out of God's grace." When a card showed as reversed, the reader presumed that anger, lust, pride, sloth, gluttony, envy, or covetousness was influencing the primary energy indicated in the card. Which of these influences was the problem was more than likely determined by intuition and the content of the reading itself. In this way, if a client had a very good card which was modified by a reversed energy, they were viewed as slightly off the path. If they had a very bad card that was reversed they were seen as deeply in trouble.

## Contemporary Perspectives on Reversed Cards

More recently, reversed cards have come to mean more than to demonstrate someone's internal struggle with evil. The primary reason for this is a change in cultural perception regarding what it means to be "In God's grace" and how energies and reversed energies might both occur and express themselves. Obviously, the world view of the typical Tarot reader has changed a great deal since the Middle Ages. The most striking change is that the modern reader recognizes that where human nature is concerned, it is perfectly possible for both good and bad energies to be suppressed. To the modern Tarot reader, there are two key areas of influence that may cause a card's energies to be reversed: environmental factors and psychological factors.

## Environmental Factors and Reversals

Environmental factors usually boil down to either clarity or timing. Often, we will find that there is so much going on in our environment that our attention is diverted away from an event or energy. We simply do not recognize it until someone points it out and then we say to ourselves "oh yeah I HAVE been thinking that," or "she IS acting in that way, isn't she?" In these cases, a card which embodies that energy may show as reversed, indicating that the event or impulse in question is not having its full effect because it is being lost in the crowd of our lives.

The other main environmental factor that may cause a card to be reversed is timing. Tarot, by definition, picks up energies that are present and future possibilities for the client. This causes one of the main reasons for cards to become reversed. Often a card will show reversed when energy is present, but for whatever reason cannot obviously express itself in the current environment. Often this is because the energy is there spiritually but it is not yet time for it to appear physically. Examples of this are found in: people who are about to fall in love (they are "putting out the vibe" but they have yet to meet the person); ideas and creative projects which are still gestating; and events which require several different energies or people to come together at the right time in order to express themselves.

## Psychological Factors and Reversals

This concept can best be explained by looking at Carl Jung's concept of the Shadow side of self. According to Jung, we all have a side to our personalities that contains the psychological makeup and impulses which are part of our true self, but which we do not want to accept as part of ourselves for one reason or another. Typically, these impulses are rejected and sent to the "shadow" part of our personalities because they are seen for some reason to represent a threat.

The key here is how the concept of threat is understood. Jung fathered an expansive psychological movement that looks at this question in depth. I cannot hope to explain the whole field of psychology and the workings of the shadow self within the scope of this book. What I can do is give you some examples so that you might begin to recognize where experiences and education you have already had touch on these matters. One example that many of you may recognize is the concept of the dysfunctional family. Many children have grown up in homes where the parents were unable to properly look after themselves and their own emotional needs. These parents were therefore unable to help their children learn how to express emotions in a healthy manner. If you watch talk shows you will see this portrayed time and time again. What interests us as Tarot readers about this concept is that the emotions that such children struggle with do not go away and is very present psychically whether or not the client is aware of them. These influences can often show up as reversed cards in a reading. As such, the reversed card will show a desire or aspect of personality that the client does not believe on a deep level it is okay to have and express. These energies may seem to the reader to be healthy or they may seem to the reader to be troublesome, but the client will always see them as troublesome in these instances.

A good example of this is the reversed Strength card. It may appear to the reader that strength is a very good thing, while to the client strength may seem threatening on a deep level even though they appear on the surface to want to be stronger and more independent. When as a reader you find you are getting mixed or confusing messages from a client it is usually quite helpful to take a careful look at any reversed cards that may be present in the reading.

## Distinguishing Between Environmental and Psychological Interpretations

Recognizing whether a card is reversed for environmental or psychological reasons is much easier than you might think. The clues are usually found in carefully studying what the card looks like when shown reversed. The symbols and artistic details that stand out in a card when you are looking at it upright are very different than the symbols and artistic details which draw the eye when it is carefully examined in the reversed position.

Cards that are reversed due to environmental considerations will closely mimic other cards in a spread in terms of coloring and symbolic detail. For example, if you look at the Empress reversed you will notice that the pumpkin and other fruit at her feet are quite noticeable. Upright they blend in to the overall picture and are not nearly as striking. If the King of Pentacles or other cards with an emphasis on harvest type images were placed in spread positions around the reversed Empress, this might suggest a visual connection. This is purely a matter of intuition and interpretation of course, but that is what Tarot is about. Briefly put if you feel that a reversed card closely reminds you of other cards in a spread, then it is connected to those cards and the reason for the reversal is likely environmental in nature.

Cards that are reversed for psychological reasons will often appear to stand apart from the rest of the reading, or will be visually much more eye catching and dominant than the cards around it. Often readers will be temporarily confused because they look at the overall spread and don't see how the card fits the overall story. This is when you know you are encountering a card that is reversed for psychological reasons.

Both when working with spreads and working with individual cards the real key to why a card is reversed lies in how the client feels about the card. Environmental cards usually cause one to feel a slight sense of expectancy and or an "AH HA." Psychological cards tend to be a tad bit confusing and uncomfortable, often causing a person to want to forget about them or gloss over them and move to other parts of the reading.

## Exercise 8A: Interpreting Reversed Cards

For this exercise, it is important that you have done the exercises in lessons one and two. If you have not, go back and do them before you attempt this one.

Refer to your Tarot journal or notes in this text and choose the same card or cards you chose in lesson one to examine and write down what you noticed about the card. This card (or cards) should be the same one you also intuitively interpreted in lesson two.

For this exercise, simply repeat the exercises in lesson one and two with the same card, only looking at it and interpreting it Reversed. Do not pick up the card and turn it around upright to get a better look. Make sure this entire exercise is done looking at the card upside down.

Specifically notice such things as what symbols stand out (they may or may not be the same symbols that stand out when you view the card upright.) Also notice what your eye focuses on and what your eye skims over. Notice if the sense of the scene or the story of the card changes when you look at it reversed.

Then pick out any key symbols you notice or any strong emotional reactions and create a meaning. You can compare it later with traditional meanings of the reversed card, and with the ideas expressed in this chapter about what reversals mean. The point for now is to let your own internal sense of what the reversed card might mean bubble up to the surface of your awareness. Take careful and detailed notes about what you see and experience.

_____

_____

_____

_____

_____

_____

_____

_____

_____

_____

_____

_____

Set aside the cards and come back to this exercise on a different day. It is important to wait at least a few hours between sessions. The reason for repeating the exercise is that reversed cards are often emotionally challenging since they speak about various blockages to the energy flowing smoothly. You may get stuck or not see enough to be useful the first time, but if you keep coming back to the card you will get a sense of what it means to you.

Now simply re-read the entries you made for the card upright and the entries you made for the card reversed. Take a few minutes and journal about the comparison and contrast and anything that comes to mind.

_____
_____
_____
_____
_____
_____
_____
_____
_____
_____
_____
_____

Finally, you can take a moment to look up some traditional meanings for the card both upright and reversed. Do those meanings make sense to you? Can you see where in the symbolism on the card those meanings and ideas are expressed? Can you easily understand and remember the traditional meanings? Is there some aspect of the meanings that you missed or disagree with personally?

## Reversed Card Exercise Using the Five of Pentacles

When the Five of Pentacles is reversed it seems less coherent and more chaotic than upright. Upright it seems like a sad scene, but there is a sense of hope inside the church or whatever building has the stained glass. Upside down the window and the figures and the snow all seem like different pictures pasted one on top of other. The crutches really stand out visually upright; they do not show up as much when the card is reversed. The window looks more like a door than a window now. Also, the figures are now moving to the left instead of the right. I associate the left with past, so it seems like they are moving backwards instead of making any progress.

# Lesson Nine

# An Overview of the Major Arcana

- The Major Arcana: Journey of the Fool
- Magician- Chariot: Spiritual and Practical Skill
- Exercise 9A- Influential Teachers
- Strength-Temperance: Self-Knowledge and Exploration
- Exercise 9B- Times of Personal Transformation
- Devil-World: Surrender and Enlightenment
- Exercise 9C- Defining Moments and Rites of Passage
- The Ever-Traveling Seeker: The Fool
- Exercise 9D- Embracing Foolishness
- Seeing the Tableau as a Map vs. a Set of Directions
- Your Personal Journey the Major Arcana
- Exercise 9E- Entering a Card

# The Major Arcana: Journey of the Fool

A simple way to understand the Major Arcana is to view them as representations of the personal transformation and spiritual rites of passage that give meaning and context to all practical life skills that are depicted in the Minor Arcana.

The Major Arcana are symbolic pictures of those moments in life when suddenly and irrevocably everything changes for us. Sometimes these spiritual openings are ecstatic, like when we realize for the first time that we are in love, and sometimes they are traumatic like when we witness a devastating historical event. In either case they are the moments that change our understanding of ourselves and the world around us, and they offer us an opportunity to strengthen our spirituality.

Because of their archetypal nature, the Major Arcana are much easier for most people to understand at first glance than the Minor Arcana. At a deep level, their energies are familiar to us and we intuitively understand them without explanation. If you doubt this ask a friend who is unfamiliar with Tarot to look at the Hermit card, or the Sun card and tell you if they can get a sense of what it means. The "wise old man" and the victories of youth are part of our spiritual and cultural experience. We all understand them at a deep level, even when we think we do not understand them at all. There are levels upon levels of deeper meanings, and more subtle growth depicted within these images, but the initial gateway to learning seems to be left wide open. Even a surface perusal of the Major Arcana can set us on a powerful spiritual and intuitive journey.

The most exciting offering the Major Arcana has for us is not how they work as individual cards, but what they have to say about how those experiences fit together and provide a collective meaning. The Major Arcana, when viewed together in numerical order, provide an outstanding map of the spiritual experience. Understanding this map allows us to more fully integrate what we have already learned, and consciously prepare for what we still need to learn as we make our way through the journey of enlightenment, often referred to as the journey of The Fool.

The Journey of The Fool is the story of every man and every woman. The Fool represents both the person at the beginning of the journey to enlightenment and the person who has reached his or her spiritual destination. Each of the other Major Arcana cards represents a life changing event which draws the Fool along the journey towards self-understanding and close relationship with the Spiritual.

In order to really understand this journey, you will want to see it. So, take a moment to stop reading this lesson and go get your cards and spread them out in the following manner: Lay the cards out in three rows of seven cards, each in numerical order from 1-21. Place The Fool (number 0) above the three rows.

# The Fool's Tableau

| Magician | Priestess | Empress | Emperor | Hierophant | Lovers | Chariot |

| Strength | Hermit | Wheel | Justice | Hanged Man | Death | Temperance |

| Devil | Tower | Star | Moon | Sun | Judgment | World |

This map is sometimes referred to as the Tarot Tableau. It is a simple yet powerful meditation and spiritual study tool. When we look at the Tableau, we see that there is a story implicit in the way the cards follow one another and seem to relate or interact. It is the story of the Fool setting off to discover the world and moving through the lessons that each card represents one by one in order.

The structure of this map, using three rows of seven cards each, with the Fool on top as an independent card is significant. Each row represents a different level of understanding the world around us and the different lessons we need to learn in order to find our spiritual core within this world. More importantly each row represents a different method of learning and a different approach to the sacred. Just as it is more intuitively powerful to begin our exploration of the Minor Arcana by really understanding what the suits mean before we delve into individually numbered cards, it is highly effective to begin looking at the Major Arcana by trying to understand the collective meaning of the three rows of seven, before delving more deeply into the individual archetypes.

## The First Row

### *Magician through Chariot: Spiritual and Practical Skill*

This first tier of the Fool's Tableau represents an approach to spirituality and to life that is oriented around learning from others. It is the stage of mastering the tools and developing the skills we will need in order to accomplish our goals and tasks. It is also the stage of the journey where we begin to see different approaches to spirituality and explore different uses of power. This row can also represent the first passage into adulthood, or the first level of competence in any art form or technology. If you look carefully at the first row of seven cards, and compare that row to the other two, you may notice these themes and many others.

This is a row where the cards depict well defined characters in mostly static scenes. In many decks, more cards from this row show characters in still poses looking directly out of the card and at the observer than in any other row in the Tableau. The relative straightforwardness and simplicity of the characters is a reflection of the lessons they are teaching the Fool. This level of the journey is about taking a moment to stand still and look around. It is about discovering your own place in the world. It is where you begin to understand that the simple facts of daily life and your surroundings hold tremendous spiritual and psychic secrets. Careful observation of life, and of the cards, will reveal that although things may seem simple and straightforward, there always seem to be contradictions and exceptions to any lesson learned.

Taken as a whole, the first row of the Tarot seems to play with the idea of polarity and opposites. The male/female pairs of Magician/Priestess and Empress/Emperor are followed (in Waite Based decks at least) with two very different cards. The rather stuffy and Christian looking "Hierophant" (in itself a pun and a contradiction) sits right next to the Lovers. The final card in this row is the Chariot that is an exquisite study in paradox and opposites. It is within this garden of opposites that the Fool first begins to explore the spiritual implications of knowledge and power. The Fool begins to ask who has authority and why, and what the rules and expectations are around using influence. The Fool also begins to wonder how she/he can maintain a place in the practical world through actions and talents without losing the sense of spirituality and meaning.

At this stage in the journey the spiritual lessons and rights of passage that the Fool experiences are both personal and strongly connected to the skills necessary for living in normal society. What you do not find in this row are the human states of awareness and virtues depicted in the second row, or the unconfined forces of nature shown in the final row. Cards like the Tower (which is sometimes called The Lightening) and The Sun from the third row clearly take us beyond the scope of human control or achievement. So too do cards from the second row. Cards from the other rows can be seen as ways of being or of understanding that arise from within the self, or from forces of pure nature and spirit, while cards from the first row such as The Magician and The Chariot seem to imply a lesson coming from outside the self and from the process of trying to relate the self to the realities of living with others.

## Exercise 9A: An Influential Teacher

The best way to fully appreciate the spiritual and practical insights that the Fool can share with us as she/he travels this first level of the journey is to experience it. Take a moment to experiment with the following exercise and record your experiences and observations in the spaces provided before you continue on to learn about the next two levels.

1) As with all Tarot work, start by clearing your mind, grounding and setting sacred space.

2) Take a moment to look at all 7 cards together in a row. Notice everything you can about the color, design and composition of the cards. Write down the things you notice that the seven cards have in common, and all the ways in which they contrast.

_____
_____
_____
_____
_____
_____
_____
_____
_____
_____
_____
_____

3) Now, set the cards aside for a moment and think about the people who have positively affected your life. Choose one individual that, for you personally, is a spiritual teacher, role model, and an example of right living.

_____
_____
_____
_____
_____
_____

4) Once you have selected your person, write down his or her name and then a list of all the skills and spiritual knowledge you have seen them put into practice, or which they have taught you about directly.

_____
_____
_____
_____
_____
_____
_____
_____
_____
_____
_____
_____

5) When your list feels complete, take a moment to write down your own name and under it a list of all the qualities, attitudes and skills you think you would need to develop in yourself in order to be more like this person.

_____
_____
_____
_____
_____
_____
_____
_____
_____
_____
_____
_____

6) Now take a moment and think about how you already have those same skills and qualities in your life and are already expressing them. Write also about how you would like to further express or develop those same qualities.

_____
_____
_____
_____
_____
_____

7) Finally, return to looking at the row of seven cards. Compare the details of artistry and symbolism in the cards to your lists and choose **one** of the seven cards to best describe the person, skills, and aspects of yourself you have been journaling about. When you are ready, summarize your discoveries by creating a meaning for the Major Arcana card you chose.

_____
_____
_____
_____
_____
_____
_____
_____
_____
_____
_____
_____
_____

## The Second Row

***Strength through Temperance: Self-Knowledge and Exploration***

This second tier of the Fool's Tableau represents an approach to spirituality and to life that centers on a strong desire to explore within and "know thy self." Here the Fool begins to question her relationship with herself and learn from herself. She begins testing the possibilities and power of her own psychic and spiritual energy. It is the stage of seeking self-knowledge and learning about values and beliefs, failure and forgiveness. This is also the stage of the journey where we begin to accept ambiguity and uncertainty as a normal part of the spiritual path, and to seek wisdom from our own experiences. Here the Fool gives up the desire to find or be an expert and learns instead to trust himself and to focus on the lessons and experiences before him.

This row can also represent the passage into middle adulthood, and the level of mastery in any art form or technology that creates confidence and allows for practical experimentation. Personal exploration of the second row of seven cards often leads to noticing certain themes in the artwork and characters on the cards. This is an exploration of the emotional, internal self.

One of the first things that distinguishes the second row of the Tableau from the first is the titles on the cards. Whereas in the first row the names are mostly titles of individuals such as the Magician and the Hierophant, in the second row the names seem to refer more to qualities and experiences. This is the row of Strength and Temperance and Justice, which are concepts that relate more to moral forces or ways of being than they are to simple rules of society, skills, and accomplishments. These are qualities that we can only understand externally once we have taken the time to develop them within ourselves.

It is also the row of Death and The Wheel of Fortune, which represent the fundamental rights of passage the Fool must experience in order to find her own truth. After all, the trials of unexpected circumstance, and the loss felt at the death of a loved one or even the death of a part of our own identity, is what leads us to turn within and seek a deeper truth.

The two cards that do indicate titles for individuals are also interesting. The Hermit and The Hanged Man receive their title and their meaning from the fact that they are characters that are defined by their separation from normal society. These are characters on a quest of an entirely personal and private nature. Unlike the Emperor or even the Charioteer (another name for the Chariot) who gain their significance from their responsibility to society, the Hermit and the Hanged Man gain their significance from their willingness to step away from society. Clearly the task for the Fool is no longer to stand still and look around, but rather to look deep within.

In addition to looking within, the Fool is being explicitly invited to risk experiencing the unusual or the unknown. Compared with the teachers that the Fool meets in the first row, those in the second row seem more active, and more directly engaged in mysterious or even perplexing activity. The second row depicts characters handling lions, climbing mountains with lanterns, hanging upside down by one foot, and magically mixing fire and water (many versions of Temperance). Even the characters representing everyday occurrence are those representing Death and Justice, those things that might happen every day, but still fill us with fear and uncertainty. And then there is The Wheel of Fortune, not a "character" at all but instead an intriguing vision or puzzle.

The self knowledge, exploration, and spiritual riddles depicted in the second row are powerful invitations for the Fool to begin discovering the authentic self and allowing this self to open up to a spiritual sense or understanding his or her destiny.

## Exercise 9B: Times of Personal Transformation

Take a moment to experiment with the following exercise and record your experiences and observations before you continue on to learn about the last row of the Tableau.

1) As with all Tarot work start by clearing your mind, grounding and setting sacred space.

2) Take a moment to look at all 7 cards together in a row. Notice everything you can about the color, design and composition of the cards. Notice if the observations made in this book about the themes in the row hold true or not for the deck you are using. Look also to see if there are additional themes and trends hidden in the artwork for these seven cards in your deck. Write down a list of all the things you notice that the seven cards have in common, and all the ways in which they contrast.

3) Now, set the cards aside for a moment and think about the periods in your life when you have undergone the most significant personal change. Think of the times when not only your relationships and activities changed, but also your priorities, attitudes, and self perceptions. Choose the period of time that you are still most effected by or curious about to focus on for this exercise. Once you have selected your time of personal history, take time and write down everything you can remember from that time. Write about people, events, emotions, environments, everything.

4) When you are done describing the time, write about how you as a person changed during that period and what you learned about yourself.

_____
_____
_____
_____
_____
_____
_____
_____

5) Now take a moment and write a paragraph describing how your life now is different because of the ways you personally changed.

_____
_____
_____
_____
_____
_____
_____
_____
_____
_____
_____

6) Finally, return to looking at the row of seven cards. Compare the details of artistry and symbolism in the cards to the feelings and experiences you have been exploring. Is there a card that seems to capture the essence of your transformation? Is there a card that seems to offer insight or suggestions for dealing with your transformation or future times like it? See if you can choose a card that seems relevant to your experiences and take the time to really study the details in that card. Explore the card in whatever way seems best to you. When you are ready summarize your discoveries by creating a meaning for this particular Major Arcana card.

_____

_____

_____

_____

_____

_____

_____

_____

_____

_____

_____

_____

_____

_____

_____

_____

_____

_____

# The Third Row

*Devil through The World: Surrender and Enlightenment*

Finally, the third tier of the Fool's Tableau represents a willingness to go beyond what we learn from others and what we learn from ourselves to the point where we learn directly from Spirit. The trials, challenges, and riddles presented in this row represent the opportunity we all have to come to terms with the forces of nature and the cosmos and find our place as an integral part of all creation. In this row we touch the primal, uncivilized, and chaotic side of ourselves and of the world and simultaneously encounter the transcendent, ethereal, and enlightened. This row can also represent the journey into old age, or the type of true mastery that allows the artist to become a vehicle for a larger message that seems to come directly from Spirit. A careful look at this last row provides many startling contrasts and compelling themes.

In the final row of the Tableau, the Fool has entered a new territory and will be required to explore a new way of seeking enlightenment. This is a realm of cosmic forces. The lessons here come not from the Fool understanding the world or even understanding himself. The lessons here arise from the willingness of the Fool to experience Spirit and be transformed by the Divine. In many decks, this transition is marked with more characters that are naked and a much greater emphasis on landscape and natural surrounding than in the other rows.

This is also a row of great force and power. Whether it is the life-altering moment of lightening striking the Tower or the steady tidal pull of the Moon, this row speaks of those forces that shape and affect us in both obvious and subtle ways. The last row is the testing ground for the Fool.

What is the Fool going to do about that Devil character? When the trumpet in Judgment blows what part of her/him is going to rise up and be born? It is time for the Fool to take action and make choices based on what she/he has learned above. It is also a time of growing into enlightenment. The Fool is showing us the way through some of our toughest lessons.

# Exercise 9C: Defining Moments and Rites of Passage

Take a moment to experiment with the following exercise and record your experiences and observations in your Tarot Journal and in the spaces provided as before.

1) As with all Tarot work start by clearing your mind, grounding and setting sacred space.

2) Take a moment to look at all 7 cards together in a row. Notice everything you can about the color, design and composition of the cards. Notice if the observations made in this text about the themes in the row hold true or not for the deck you are using. Look also to see if there are additional themes and trends hidden in the artwork for these seven cards in your deck. Write down a list of all the things you notice that the seven cards have in common, and all the ways in which they contrast. Challenge yourself to notice and record every scrap of detail possible.

_____
_____
_____
_____
_____
_____
_____
_____

3) Now, set the cards aside for a moment. Take a moment to review your life and see if you can choose five defining moments when an event happened that changed who you are and how you see the world. Choose different types of events.

_____
_____
_____
_____
_____
_____
_____
_____
_____
_____
_____
_____
_____
_____
_____
_____
_____
_____
_____

4) Once you have selected events, take a few moments to muse on which of those events seem to have set in motion choices or attitudes that are strongly affecting your current life. Choose a single event that you are interested in exploring further. Take a few minutes to write about the event and how it has affected your personality and your life choices.

6) When you feel complete with your event description, take a moment to pretend that you are a wise old guru and you are using the event you described as a parable to teach an important spiritual lesson to a group of eager young followers. What is the spiritual lesson that was made available to you through that event? Why is it an important or valuable spiritual lesson to learn? Write until you feel that you have discovered and or explained your insight fully.

7) Finally, return to looking at the row of seven cards. Compare the details of artistry and symbolism in the cards to the feelings and experiences you have been exploring. Is there a card that seems to capture the essence of the spiritual lesson you were describing? Is there a card that seems to offer insight or suggestions for dealing with similar events or happenings in the future? See if you can choose a card that seems to depict the spiritual nature of the event you chose. Explore the card in whatever way seems best to you. When you are ready, summarize your discoveries by creating a meaning for this particular Major Arcana card.

_____
_____
_____
_____
_____
_____
_____
_____
_____
_____
_____

## The Ever-Traveling Seeker: The Fool

After you have explored the three rows of the Fool's Tableau, take a moment to return to the Fool. She (or he of course) is the Alpha/Omega, the seeker, the infinite circle, the moment between ignorance and learning. The Fool represents that exciting time when you don't yet know what it is you do not know. The Fool also represents the experience of being indistinguishable from and connected to all life. It is a powerful card to take the time to fully experience.

# Seeing the Tableau as a Map vs. a Set of Directions

It is important to remember that the Tableau is a map, not a set of directions. Looking at a map allows us to see the entire territory and decide where we want to proceed. We are free to move in any direction we wish. Unlike a set of directions that has a specific beginning and ending destination, the journey of the Fool is a circle. When we come to the "end" of this journey and the World, we discover that the path is not linear and we are moved back to the beginning and the Fool.

The circular journey of the Fool is a rather chaotic one at that. While the Fool does indeed proceed through the different lessons in the Tableau, she does not necessarily do so in a linear fashion. She may stay in one place for a long time, and then suddenly jump to a new one, only to return to where she started. Or she may proceed steadily along the path in a single direction. As she travels through the rows she is also experiencing the columns in the Tableau. Every time a lesson is being learned at one level it touches slightly on lessons that may seem to be much deeper or much more to the surface of where we think we are, but which are really simply different faces of the same thing. In this way, every time the Fool is learning from the Magician, she is also learning Strength and the Devil, and every time we find ourselves in the Moon card we may also find need for the lessons we have learned in the Emperor and in Justice. Like the Tarot, the natural world, the Divine, and everything in it is interconnected. You cannot affect one part of your being without also affecting others.

The spiraling and dancing movement of the Fool is characteristic of all of us as we grow on our spiritual journey. We all spiral through this journey many, many times. We move forward and backwards and up and down and in a circle, but we are always moving and always learning. That is after all the core of the Fool's Journey: personal discovery.

# Your Personal Journey: The Major Arcana

As you work with the above, it is easy to see how the Major Arcana tells a story that is at the same time about us individually as well as about all of us collectively. You will also notice that the above exercise only brushes the surface of the meaning and insight available in these cards. Below is an exercise that can be done with any Tarot card to gain deeper insight and meaning, but seems to have particular power when applied to the Major Arcana.

## Exercise 9D: Gaining Deeper Insight on a Card

1) If you are intrigued about a particular Major Arcana card, you may choose it to do this exercise, or you may choose a Minor Arcana to explore more deeply in this way.

2) To do this properly, start by taking a careful, purposeful look at the card before you write down everything you can think of about the visual details of the card. This exercise only counts if you uncover clear, visual details that you could point out or draw for someone else. (For example, you cannot draw "expansive" as that is a feeling, but you can draw wide open arms or rays of yellow etc.)

_____
_____
_____
_____
_____
_____
_____
_____

3) You may do the second half of this exercise immediately following the first part, or on a different day. It does not matter. For the second part, you must have a place where you can get very comfortable and have at least a half hour completely without interruption. When you are ready get comfortable and close your eyes. Do the simple grounding exercise from lesson one, and imagine yourself surrounded by loving and protective energy. You may wish to invite your Spiritual Source to join you and guide and protect you during this exercise. When you feel fully relaxed, grounded, and as though you are in a sacred space, imagine the card in as vivid detail as you can. If your mind wanders do not worry, simply bring your attention back to the mental exercise of constructing the card. When the card is very clear in your mind's eye, make it bigger and brighter in your mind. Continue doing this and imagine the card in front of you, standing upright on its edge. Allow the card to grow to approximately the size of a doorway filled with light and brilliant color. You might find it easier to envision a movie screen. Either way, when this is quite clear, state in your mind that you are going to visit the card in order to learn what it has to teach you, and step through your astral doorway. Be sure to look to your right and left and discover what is in the landscape of the card that you could not see when looking at it through the "window" or doorway of the card.

4) After taking some time to explore, repeat your mental intention to learn what the card has to teach you and quietly wait. After a moment, if there are "characters" in the card, you may ask them any questions you might have. You may also find yourself simply sitting. When you feel that you are finished (and you will feel that very clearly when it is over) offer a gift to the card from your own love and affection. You may also wish to create a mental symbol or gift if it seems appropriate. Wait one final time for any further

information and then mentally turn around and step through the doorway, bringing your mind's focus back into your body. It is important to take the time to mentally reverse the process, to shrink the card back down, allow the colors to become normal and mentally return the card to its place on the table or in the deck before opening your eyes.

5) After your eyes open sit quietly and take 10 deep breaths. Look at the ceiling, wiggle your toes, sniff the air and see what smells you detect, listen for far off noises, and make a purposeful reconnection with your surroundings. Do not skip these steps, as it is very important to gradually return your awareness rather than to just jump from the meditative mind to the active mind.

6) Once you have fully "come back into your body" write down everything you remember, whether it makes sense or not. You will find either immediately or with time that some very powerful insights were gained with this exercise.

_____
_____
_____
_____
_____
_____
_____
_____
_____
_____
_____
_____

# Lesson Ten

## Working with Meditation and Set Interpretation
## The Major Arcana Cards: Fool-Chariot

- Taking It Deeper: Matching Insight to Personal Experience
- The Fool
- The Magician
- The High Priestess
- The Empress
- The Emperor
- The Hierophant
- The Lovers
- The Chariot

# Taking It Deeper: Matching Insight to Personal Experience

The next three lessons are about your own exercises and experiences. For this one, separate out the Fool and the Major Arcana cards 1-7.

Then each day, set aside some time for study, and choose one of the seven cards at random. Read the predictive meaning and meditation listed here. Take a moment to journal about any thought or opinion that the information brings up. Also take a moment to really look at the card(s) and see if you can see what symbols and images in the cards I based my theories on. Journal about that, too.

Then set the card aside and go about your day. At the end of the day come back and look at the information written here and your personal journaling as well. Reflect on your day and decide what was accurate, what was not accurate and what real life experiences you had that taught you new ways of looking at the "meanings" of the card as you understood them in the morning. Write about your impressions, questions, and experiences.

The next day choose randomly from the remaining cards until you have done this exercise with each of the first seven cards of the Major Arcana, including the Fool.

# The Fool

***Predictive Meaning***: Today is a great day to go out and "Seize the Day," a great day to take risks, try new things, and start projects that are near and dear to your heart. This is a day about doing your own thing so do not create conflict by insisting friends and family understand and support what you are up to. For today, focus on doing what you love, and go out into the world and create new opportunities for yourself. Rejoice in your uniqueness. Today is not a day to worry about major decisions or the future much. You will only make yourself more confused and not really settle anything, so trust that things will work out and instead live your life as if you had everything you ever wanted in this present moment. When we live our lives as if they are the ones we want to live, things change and we realize our goals are manifesting around us. This is the card of new beginnings, spiritual journeys, and being able to tap into that inner knowing that there is something more to this life beyond the normal physical.

***Meditation***: Many people consider the Fool to be such an important card that it represents the entire deck all by itself. And in many, many ways it does. The figure of a young Man or Woman (or androgynous figure) stepping lightly along on a powerfully important journey is the image of us all. The Fool journeys forward with a pole over the shoulder, a small bundle tied to the pole, a dog at her side and a flower in her hand. The Fool is the ultimate figure of the hero out to seek fortune. In most decks, this hero is also poised to step right off a cliff into the unknown, but we suspect that he will be fine and even benefit in some mysterious way from his "fall." After all the sudden plunge into the unknown is where all great adventure stories and spiritual stories begin. So, this card is inviting you to step out on your own adventure! Are you ready? There is really not much to say but to invite you to do whatever it is your heart is calling you most to do, because that is likely your soul's purpose.

# Magician

***Predictive Meaning***: Today is a day to look carefully at the tools on your table and the plans in your head and decide exactly what it is that you are setting out to create. Our intentions, thoughts, and beliefs can indeed create reality, but when was the last time you took a moment to have a long hard look about what it is you are really creating and why? You have more power and more options than you think. Things that you see as obstacles could actually be important tools and if you are loyal to your own self and passionate in your quest you will find just how to use those tools for your best benefit. You have the ability to use the tools on the table to make your own reality.

***Meditation***: The Magician has many tricks and many tools to show us. Perhaps the most interesting of which is "why is he pointing like that?" Many of you will have heard that the Magician teaches the lesson of "As above, so below," a belief that many religion's hold which means that God's will manifests in physical reality, and that we can make that energy manifest here on earth because we are made in the image of God. We can make heaven right here on earth, or hell if we choose to. But what does that really mean for us as individuals, and perhaps more importantly what do we do with that information? The Magician is clearly involved in a creative activity and he is clear about his intentions. Are we? Do we really have a clear idea of what we are doing now and what we hope to gain by it?

Some of these answers can be found by exploring the echo cards, the two cards that fall directly below the Magician, when you lay out the Major Arcana in three rows of seven cards as described in the Tableau. These are cards that can echo meaning and illuminate new insights for each other. Each set of three can be taken as a spiritual lesson that we can decode by careful study of the cards individually and as a group. In this case we have Strength (in most modern decks) and the Devil. In fact, in many decks the Devil card is drawn in such a way as to directly parody the body position of the Magician, and Strength picks up many elements from the Magician too, including the particular flowers around her and the infinity symbol over her head.

When we look at our own creative process, try to discern the lesson of "As above, so below." With a little help from Strength and the Devil cards, we find ourselves with many new questions to ask and riddles to solve. Where is false ego or imbalanced desire involved in our creations? Do we understand fully our own strength, power, and ability to be in right relationship with the world? Is there a part of us, perhaps buried deep in our sub-conscious, that is working against our best efforts?

Can we find how to tame it with love and communication instead of repression and dominance? At least these are some of the questions I find when contemplating the Magician. What questions do you find? Take a moment to do a ritual, look up some traditional card meanings, journal, meditate, or do whatever else it is you need to do to find your own understanding of the mysteries of the Magician.

## High Priestess

***Predictive Meaning***: Today is a day to delve into the depths of your intuition and emotion. It is also a day to allow yourself to learn from the unexpected, especially the unexpected within yourself. Be sure to get enough rest and also be sure to allow yourself to keep your own secrets. Today is not a good day to try to explain your motives. Instead do the best you can and trust that things will work out. Luck is good today and you will also find "behind the scenes help." Also, this is a terrific day for writing, meditating, and spiritual pursuits of all kinds. She holds the scrolls of all there is, and all there ever will be, so do understand that the knowledge is there for us, if we still our minds and allow it to come to us.

***Meditation:*** There are many mysteries kept and tended by the High Priestess, but perhaps the most interesting of all is "what's behind the curtain?" That is, what is behind the curtain of our own self-image? What lies at the core of who we are and at the core of our beliefs? The key to finding some type of trail to follow to specific and concrete insights can be found in the "echo" cards. The High Priestess is echoed below by the Hermit and the Tower. So, we can ask ourselves not only what it is that we hide behind our own curtain, (for better or for worse, The Priestess likes to remind us that some things are best when kept private) but also where is our flame of inspiration? Where is it that we can contact our inner self?

Why do we sometimes keep that light of inspiration behind the curtain? Is it serving us well to do so or not? Also, why is it that we let that inspiration get off track and lead us into false security or unhealthy pursuits? Ask yourself about these things and how they manifest for you in daily life and you can be sure that the Priestess will reveal many mysteries.

# Empress

*Predictive Meaning:* This is a great time to celebrate community, abundance, and all forms of the Harvest. This is a terrific day to share your creative ideas, hobbies, and playful side with friends and family. A sense of re-birth and new options and freedoms in the physical world may prevail today. It is also an important day to show thanks and give back to your community through volunteer activities, simple kindness to strangers, or making a gift of your unique talents. You have the ability to create all things, as we are all a part of the Creative Mind of the Universe. Most of all it is a day to simply enjoy being in the physical world.

*Meditation:* The card depicts a fertile "Earth Mother" sitting outside amongst the grains with a crown of stars on her head, a heart shaped pillow next to her, and an abundance of feminine symbolism. She asks us questions about our role in our greater communities and about how we can create and enjoy divine abundance by simply being who and what we naturally are. She is also here to show us that sometimes creativity and creation are not achieved by awareness, either conscious like the Magician, or sub-conscious like the Priestess. Sometimes the natural result of engaging with life is creating more life. This is the process of simply accepting the spark of Divine Spirit to come through us and be expressed. Sometimes just being is enough. (After all a pregnant woman does not "direct" the growth of her child. It is simply a natural process which she experiences without controlling.)

The questions the Empress asks us here are simple. Can we accept? Are we really able to "be here, be now" or are we still caught in the process of action, judgment and more action? Are we ready to assume creative responsibility for our lives and circumstances we manifest with our desires? Do we accept the full spectrum of creativity or limit it to only a few 'acceptable' expressions?

The echo cards here are quite powerful: The Wheel of Fortune and The Star. The Wheel of Fortune is reminding us that the Empress represents love and creation- but that her serenity and stillness should in no way be taken to mean that she is predictable or controlled. She is the mediator between chaos and order, form and force. She contains it all and rejects none of it. Can we do that? How comfortable are we with the inevitable chaos, confusion, and even pain that comes with all growth and creation? Are we limiting ourselves by a need to make things understandable and orderly? Or are we too comfortable with chaos? Are we mistaking all change for good change and all pain for growing pains? How well do we mediate between order and chaos, form and force, stillness and motion, within our own lives?

The Star as an echo card for the Empress takes these concepts and reminds us to connect them back to the world around us. Most creativity has a very slow stage from pregnancy to invention, and some of the process is always internal, but that reminds us that for it to matter we must release our hold and pour the waters of our creativity back into the world. We must allow the child to become her own person, the artwork to convey messages we never knew were there and the invention to be used in ways we never dreamed. The Empress is challenging us to hold firm by never letting go, and to accept that we will from time to time find our creativity having a mysterious effect on the universe. By the same token the Star is reminding us that the Empress knows fully that she is never alone. There is always a guiding star and a helping energy to guide her on the path. The Empress is simply asking us to allow, accept, and to wait and see. Can we do as she does?

# Emperor

*Predictive Meaning:* A day to get things done, pay attention to the structures that are important in your life, and claim your power in the temporal world. This is also a time to focus on what must be preserved or cared for and what must be planned or prepared for. It is a time when ethics and long term strategic planning must be addressed and decisions must be made as to how to preserve both through concrete actions. Moving inspiration, idealism, and a love of beauty into concrete action is the goal. Today will be a very logical, cause and effect kind of day. It is a great day for business, especially entrepreneurial business. This is a day to come into your personal power and assume your role as a leader and organizer.

*Meditation:* So how do we manifest Divine will? Intent (Magician) inspiration (Priestess) and creative flow (Empress) are not enough. There is that little matter of "Right Action." The Emperor asks us questions about how to identify and hold onto actions that are well rooted in Divine Truth. The echo cards of Justice and the Moon also remind us that right action is accompanied by the need for great balance, great trust in spirit and great attention to cause and effect or "karma." In order to find our life's purpose and the actions we are truly meant to take, we also need to find our own sense of truth and justice and allow ourselves to move beyond deception and illusion and beyond to the source of Divine Law and "higher understanding." So perhaps the greatest question that the Emperor asks is "what are you going to do about it?" What do you think you personally need to do to create a personal and deep understanding of the Emperor card?

## Hierophant

***Predictive Meaning***: Today is a great day to focus on learning, teaching, and keeping up the traditions that are important to you from your culture, family group, or religion. A sense of connection to those who have gone before us and those who will come after us is important. It is also a time when it is good to remember to look outside of ourselves and try to see the world through the eyes of others. Patience, tolerance, and the realization that not all worthwhile things can be had immediately are also lessons of today. This is an important day for you to set the groundwork for your future, but do remember that sometimes miracles happen in mysterious ways and that the wisest person of all is the one that is willing to release control and admit what it is he/she does not know.

***Meditation:*** What have you learned from others that is false, hazardous, or getting in your way? What have you learned from others that is a jewel of wisdom to be cherished and examined? Can you tell the difference? These are some of the main questions of the Hierophant. This card is echoed by the Hanged Man and The Sun, two very different and powerful cards in their energies. One of the main lessons this echo gives us, and the placement of the Hierophant between the Emperor and the Lovers, is the gift of paradox. Can you tell the difference between paradox and contradiction? Is there one?

Also are you willing, like the Hanged Man, to suspend your personal sense of what is right and wrong, black and white, true and false? Are you willing to wait and get silent and seek inspiration from the Tree of Life and from life itself?

And having done that, are you ready to take what you have learned, no matter how obscure out into the light of the Sun and put it into effect in the "real world?" Pretty obscure stuff, but it is also "deep," "mystical," and highly rewarding once you get a hold of it. But it is the job of a Hierophant (which is an ancient religious title) to be an initiating Priest or Priestess, sending the questioner on a personal journey of faith and exploration. So, I invite you to decide what it all really means. If you were going to teach another about the mysteries of the Hierophant and its many meanings, how would you go about it? What do you say when you find yourself in the position of teacher?

# Lovers

***Predictive Meaning***: Today will be a day where "Divine Influence" plays a major role. Be gentle with yourself and "go with the flow" because things are happening for a reason. Likewise, today will be a day where you get to see yourself in unexpected new ways and learn more about all your own many fascinating facets of personality. You will be able to see that there are multiple choices today on how and what you focus your energy on. You will feel the "attraction of choice," knowing that you have free will to choose the life you live and the path you walk. There are glimpses of the Higher Forces at work in your life. Balance between your creative and logical sides is essential today as is careful attention to communication. What you think you hear is not always what is being said so practice active listening, double checking, and seeing the world from perspectives other than your own. Generally, a good luck day with many great opportunities and you guessed it- today is a good day for relationships, but more for deep intimacy and learning than wild parties and gratuitous sex. Enjoy the day nonetheless.

***Meditation:*** This is one of those cards that really gets people's attention because of its name. It is also quite a powerful card chock full of symbols. This card traditionally depicts a man and a woman standing naked outside with an angel looking down over the two of them. Quite often the man is looking at the woman and the woman is looking at the angel. To me this card is obviously about the nature of seeing what you want to see, of contrasts and polarity.

Clearly the Lovers card is not about a twosome, despite what immediately leaps to mind when we say the word "lovers." Here the angel is as significant or more important a player as any other character in the card. But the angel seems (as perhaps it should be an angel) omnipresent and in many decks takes up more than 1/3 of the whole card with its presence. And yet it appears that the man of the card is unaware. After all, the shadow side of the lovers can be self-absorption.

The "echo" cards for the Lovers are Death and Judgment. These are echoes that are usually pretty easy to comprehend as all of us have at some time or another had a relationship which transformed us so totally it is as if the old self died and a new one was born. In addition, judgments are the stuff of enlightenment and is old baggage weighing us down, and that is what keeps therapists in business. So, it is pretty safe to say that we are familiar with it.

# Chariot

*Predictive Meaning:* This is a day to act, to run with the choice you have made in the Lovers card, and not to let anything get in your way. If you stay motivated, nothing will stop you. This is not a day to make decisions, try instead to do further discovery/research and to dig deeper into what your options really are. It is also a day of high activity and getting things done. You will find that you have a lot of vision and creative energy today but that it takes tremendous discipline on your part to stay focused on the task at hand. Relationships may require extra tolerance both on your part and on the part of others towards you. Remember to clarify all communication and to look beyond the surface. If you do, you may find some lovely surprises and a deeper, more fulfilling connection with people. But if you take things exactly at face value today you may discover that you have misinterpreted and lost a great opportunity to connect with loved ones in a deep way.

*Meditation:* This is certainly a powerful card. For me it is a card that pulls together the energies of the Magician, Priestess, Empress, Emperor, Hierophant, and Lovers and examines what it is to try to integrate the lessons of all these cards and then take them into the real world of practical application. For this reason, this card is sometimes referred to as the "Right Use of Will" card or the "Spiritual Warrior" card.

This card is echoed by Temperance and the World. There are many lessons of balance and blending and give and take for you here. How do you think all of that can possibly be accomplished? What is the journey like for you when trying to integrate your spiritual and personal insights and "Walk your Talk?" Or are you largely being hypocritical without realizing it? Do you see anything interesting in this card that helps with that process? Do you see anything else? Be specific.

# Lesson Eleven
# A Deeper Look at the Major Arcana
# Strength through Temperance

- Strength
- The Hermit
- The Wheel of Fortune
- Justice
- Hanged Man
- Death
- Temperance

# Continued Awareness

For this week, continue the same type of exploration you did last week with the first row of 7 in the Major Arcana. Also, see if you can discover for yourself how this is a different group. How are the themes in this week's batch of cards subtly different than those from last week? Please remember that the predictive meanings and meditations supplied here are not the only meanings or meditations possible, but are simply suggestions to help you get started. Remember my authority in Tarot comes ultimately from my experience, and your authority in Tarot will come from your own experience, not from memorizing or blindly agreeing with the experiences of others, including mine.

# Strength

***Predictive Meaning:*** Today is a day to pay careful attention to balance and communication. You can get most of what you want, but you need to make a point of respectfully sticking up for yourself and being sure that you do not care for the needs of another to the detriment of yourself. Also, be sure not to assume what motivates others. Today your assessments about the character of others could actually reveal more about yourself than about them if you do not take care to listen carefully and let go of previous assumptions. At the same time, you can expect to exhibit great amounts of energy and charisma today and others will be genuinely admiring you. It is a terrific time to start or research new business ventures. It is also a great day to "clear the air" in relationships and to make plans for the future with others as long as you are respectful and attentive in your approach. Finally, be sure to take care of your health today and to enjoy both physical exercise and sensual or sensory pleasures. Just remember as you enjoy your high energy and physical expression today that the goal is balance in all things. This is not a card of exhibiting brute force, but in showing that with gentle energy you can move mountains.

***Meditation:*** Strength is asking us to learn about power. What is the difference between a destructive power in a relationship where one person is basically controlled by another, and a constructive power within a relationship where both people are enriched by the interaction? Strength suggests to us that the answer to this question lies in the mirror. We need to take the time to see that all around us is a reflection of our true self in other people and in nature. As we build respectful and meaningful relationships with others we build respect and meaning within ourselves. We need to explore concepts such as right livelihood, true love, ecology, sacred space, holistic health, and creativity with an eye to what these things can teach us about how to release our own fears and come to know and trust our deepest darkest self. We need to open up to all aspects of ourselves and to the full level of our passion in order to learn how to be all of who we are. Repression and restriction eventually lead to violence and evil. Instead, we must engage in true self-discipline, which comes from honoring and knowing all aspects of ourselves and making conscious loving choices about how we will use our mind, body, and spirit. In order to manifest anything, we must also understand that there is a part working against that very same manifestation. Fighting this part of our self will only increase its power over us. Learning about it will turn it into a powerful ally.

## The Hermit

*Predictive Meaning*: Today is a great day to trust your own opinions and instincts above those of others and to spend time on the things that you feel are important. You have the ability to tap into the wisdom of the Universe. Do not let yourself get pulled off course today by the demands of a hectic life or the needs of others. Take the time to spend some time quietly and alone and doing what is important to you. This is also a day to be sure to engage your spiritual side, and particularly to share prayers or thoughts of thanks for the many blessings you have been given. Today is also a great day to make plans, get any writing done you are planning on doing, and spend time in nature.

*Meditation:* Echoed above by the High Priestess and below by the Tower, the Hermit teaches us alot about balance and centering and the old adage that "things are not always what they appear to be." The challenge here is that we ourselves are not always what we appear to be, even to ourselves, and self-knowledge is the first key to wisdom. So, the questions for the day center upon how well do you know yourself. Are you really being, thinking, and doing what you do for the reasons you think? Or is there more to you than even you know?

Soul searching is in order when this card arises, as is the knowledge that you may have more spirit and wisdom to offer others than you think. Start listening to your heart and intuition and do not get distracted by the crumbling practical world around you. Often you will see that you are hanging on to things you do not need or really want and that you have greatness in your future of which you have previously been unaware. At least it is something you should think about a bit. What else does this card lead you to think about?

# Wheel of Fortune

***Predictive Meaning:*** There are three major keys to making today work for you:

1) Do not let yourself get distracted. Decide your priorities early in the day and stick to them.

2) Just because someone else is having a crisis does not mean that you need to have the crisis.

3) Remember, sometimes the way to success lies only through taking risks and trusting our insight.

Do not expect to have a clearly laid out plan that never deviates. Life is messy, and concrete answers are usually wrong and rarely work. Do not be afraid to trust yourself, focus on what you want, and then go for it. Don't take what is not yours, including heartache and worry, which are often needed elements of deeper spiritual growth. To take them on when they are not yours can actually be to rob someone of their spiritual opportunities. Offer help, if asked, but do so from your own center, not from caretaking mode. Today is a great day to get things done, take some time to be by yourself, and to take a moment and show gratitude for the Universe and all the gifts you are given in your life. Make a list. There are more blessings there than you may be aware of and fully accepting.

***Meditation:*** This card certainly is rich in symbolism, but the greatest image is the title of the image: The Wheel of Fortune. Many things come directly to mind when working with it. First off, if we are at the edge of the Wheel then we are more apt to feel the ups and downs of life. Life is only a Ferris Wheel when we live it from the surface. When we know who and what we are on a deep level and stick to our instincts and self-knowledge, we find ourselves moving to the center of the wheel where we are more secure from the slings and arrows of outrageous fortune. Here we can more clearly see the big picture and the overall inter-relatedness of all things. Since we have journeyed this far and have learned all the lessons up to this point, we can now take the Wheel and spin it to our advantage. We are ready to change our destiny, now empowered with our new growth.

# Justice

***Predictive Meaning:*** A great day for balance and truth. Speak and judge very carefully today, as today you will be given a chance to see the ramifications of your actions even more clearly than usual. It is however a positive and powerful opportunity. You will find that it is easier than usual to get friends and loved ones to listen to you regarding topics that are difficult to talk about. On the other hand, they may not always agree, so be sure of your willingness for true communication before you start! This is a day to balance your intuition around what you know to be true with your logical understanding of the facts. Today is an excellent day for starting new business deals and for settling old ones or outstanding conflicts. This is also a great day to think over how you will vote in local or national elections, write a letter to the editor, help a neighbor, or become involved in your larger community in any other way. The key to today is to keep a level head, get things done, mix intuition with logic, and not take every experience you have too personally. Believe it or not sometimes we are not actually the center of the Universe.

On a deeper note, this card is the first card where the Fool stops observing and begins doing, as it is the Fool himself that holds the scales and sword, weighing and measuring his former experiences, wondering if he is worthy and willing to proceed along the path.

***Meditation:*** Justice sits right in the middle of this journey. Below her is the psychic world of the Moon above her is the practical world of the Emperor, and the next numbered card after her is the Hanged Man. Clearly, she is calling for balance and for a look at the "heart of the matter" while preparing us for our first step on a highly personal initiation journey (The Hanged Man.). So, for me the question she asks is "what is the truth and what is the core issue?" To me she is about learning from the deep core of ourselves rather than learning from the outside in and we often do. Things to ask yourself when confronted with Justice are "what patterns repeat over and over again in my life?" "Do I understand them really?" "Are they healthy?" And "what deeper level do I want to go to with my life?" "Am I willing to mix logic and intuition, action and patience, in order to get there?"

# Hanged Man

***Predictive Meaning***: Change your plans for today. Whatever it is you want to accomplish, try going about it in a totally new fashion. Try new approaches and trust your instincts, but more importantly trust the Divine to see you through any unexpected challenges. You may feel stuck or think things are not exactly going your way, but have faith! The Universe is on your side and today you will have an opportunity to change your perspective and see things from a new light. This will indeed bring you good fortune in the future, although it may be several weeks (or even several years) before you understand the total picture. Today is also a day when you are likely to find help from "unexpected" allies and a day that is ideal for spending time in nature or in meditation. This is a day to contemplate the numerous feelings, concerns, and other doubts you might have encountered in the Justice card, and devise plans for addressing those issues.

***Meditation:*** The Hanged man sits directly below the Hierophant card and directly above the Sun when you look at the Tableau. He is inviting us to take what we have learned from all outside sources and turn it upside down and inside out, examining every scrap of information we have ever gathered from other people, and place it in the light of our own intuition and personal understanding. This allows us to find our own truth and shows us the way to start manifesting our creative impulses in tangible and effective ways. In order to successfully learn this system, we must discover the concept of leverage. It is often the case that pushing for a big change just creates resistance, but with the right leverage even a very small, subtle shift can lead to huge results.

In order to find out where to apply leverage in your life, look for the things you normally avoid paying attention to, and focus on them. You may find great insight there. The so-called obstacles on your journey to learning might be the actual lesson itself. The Hanged Man is in Tree Pose, a Hatha Yoga position, which is designed to help bring clarity, pose, and calmness to the individual. Take the time to retreat within and turn your question over to a Higher Power.

When we focus on the simple and small truths of our everyday experience we find the keys to unlocking our greatest potentials. When we stay focused on our truth we can see more clearly where our energy might be negating those simple and seemingly small truths. Remember, obtaining your heart's desire is no small matter, and true bliss usually requires the whole system to change. What about your present circumstance? Is it a result of "more than the sum of the parts?" How can you change yourself to see your whole world in a new way? Answer these questions and you will find that the things you see the circumstances you call obstacles more as lessons or stepping stones.

# Death

***Predictive Meaning***: Today is a day to stop repeating patterns that no longer serve you. They are not going to bring you to where you want to go, today or any other day. More effort will only lead to more problems. If whatever you are seeking has not happened by now, its not going to. You need Instead, today is a day to simply stop and cut your losses.

Once you have stopped, start to listen. You will find that people are talking about you today and the things they say may surprise you. Many of your talents and abilities are being subtly praised by those around you. Also there is great change going on around you and much of it is beyond your control. You will realize that you are not the person you used to be, and in fact are destined for far greater goals than anticipated.

Today is a day to shed that skin, remove all the people, thoughts, and habits that no longer serve you, and step into your new life. It's not an easy process, but nothing worth having ever is. So clean out the clutter in your life to make way for the transformations ahead. You are on the verge of a major breakthrough.

***Meditation:*** Placed in the column between the Lovers and Judgment, this is a card about really getting to know ourselves and acknowledging that we may not have known ourselves as well as we thought. The key here is the release of our past conceptions about ourselves and everything else and radically trust that the Divine Truth in all things will surface if we simply stay open and observant. You cannot be the new person you are designed to if you cling to old habits, thoughts, and items that no longer serve you. What personal messages do you find? Which ones are long overdue?

# Temperance

***Predictive Meaning***: Stay open to unexpected blessings and inspiration today. You will find yourself having a day in which things seem to fall into place. There may be unusual mixes of work and play activities. Friends or acquaintances you have not heard from in some time may also contact you. Be sure to listen carefully and to network. You could meet someone special or find a new job opportunity at an impromptu social event. You have the ability to blend those elements that might otherwise have been a mystery you have mastered the art of balance. You understand the adage of everything in moderation, and know that only when we live physically, emotionally, and spiritually will we gain true meaning of life.

***Meditation***: Divine Law states as above so below, as within so without. The Divine Energy of the universe requires us to give up a human understanding of nature and the events of our own lives and take a Divine Perspective. When we do this, we learn that everything happens for a reason and that everything is connected to everything else. Each atom contains within it the blueprint for all life, from the stars to the universe to the mountains to the trees. And likewise, every mountain and tree and star is nothing more than another expression of the same basic principles at work in a simple atom.

# Lesson Twelve

# A Deeper Look at the Devil through the World

- Relating to the Infinite
- The Devil
- The Tower
- The Star
- The Moon
- The Sun
- Judgment
- The World
- Exercise 12A: Developing Your Own Predictions and Meditations

# Relating to the Infinite

In our continued exploration of the Major Arcana it is important to remember that this last row is about finding our own relationship with the Universe. Once again, draw a card from this row each morning, meditate on it for 3-5 minutes, and then write your thoughts in your journal. Then come back to it again at the end of the day and see what your day helped you to understand about the card and about your own relationship with the cosmos.

# Devil

*Predictive Meaning:* Today is a day to watch your ego carefully and to make sure that you take personal responsibility for your actions. See to it that you act according to your own highest and best principles and abilities. You can learn much about your own power today by confronting your self and learning to love those parts of yourself that you see as less than perfect. We all have a darker side, elements in our past that we are not proud of, and the only way to really learn from them and overcome them is to face them head on.

*Meditation:* The Devil is quite a companion to the Magician and Strength, and a card that we should take extra care to learn from instead of dismissing as evil, scary, or simply a representation of bad things. The Devil is here to remind us that every time we work towards a goal or ideal, if it is worth anything, we will encounter resistance in others and ourselves. The Devil is here to show us where we might be self-destructive or working against our own aims. He is also here to help us slow down and understand our own fears and secrets, and the power and enormity of the changes we might be seeking to make in ourselves and our world when we set out on the journey of enlightenment.

The Devil can only be confronted and understood on the personal level so this card asks who is your Devil? What part of you is to blame when you find yourself saying or thinking "The Devil Made Me Do it" and how can the Devil be your ally and not your enemy? Is there some positive thing he can teach you if you take the time to listen?

# Tower

*Predictive Meaning:* Try to let go of your ego and relax today because you might find out that you have been wrong about something. Not to worry though, it will turn out in the long run that you are glad about the way things are turning out. So, make room for the unexpected. Try to listen to criticism honestly, and do not put too much effort into making your pet project turn out "just right." Instead, practice trust. When we feel most hopeless and frustrated is often when the Universe gives us the greatest gifts. Make room for new blessings and allow the old habits we identified in the Devil to be ousted from your life.

*Meditation:* The Tower sits directly above the High Priestess and the Hermit, both serious teachers about finding our own personal wisdom and understanding. The question with the Tower is: are you willing to take a look at the false structures in your life and let go of what does not make sense for your deepest soul self, even if it seems to be what you "need" to do in the practical world? This is a card that demands we find radical trust in our spiritual source and in our own Inner Light. We need to act from truth instead of from a strategy we have learned to use to deal with an imperfect world. If we do not make the changes that are needed to grow, often those changes are made for us in a way we otherwise may not like, so do not fight the process. It is better to resign from a job than to be fired, and the more we fight the process, the more likely our distractions will get us booted out the door. The Tower reminds us that ego has no place on the spiritual path. The Tower, which is being struck by lightning, teaches us that nothing real can be threatened, and that we need one final wake up call to see our faults and flaws, the false confidences we may be holding onto, and instead be humble.

# Star

*Predictive Meaning:* A day to celebrate the psychic and spiritual cycles of your life and to take some time to integrate and give thanks for all you have learned. This is a day to be outside and to engage your senses. Physical healing is likely, as is a sense of deep peace. You are likely to have revelations as to "why" certain challenges have been in your life. Hope is restored, trust renewed. Somehow you internally know that all situations and crises in your life will work themselves out, even if you are not sure of how that will happen.

*Meditation:* The Universe states that you cannot teach without learning, that you cannot create without destroying, and that you cannot be active without being at times passive. The Star is here to show us and to help us learn. The Star is in the third column of the Major Arcana, and is "echoed" by both The Wheel of Fortune and the Empress. Both of these cards show the progression from growth to action to faith. The Star shows us that ultimately it is the inner world of our psyche that ultimately is manifested on our journey.

# Moon

***Predictive Meaning***: Today you can expect strong emotions and even stronger impulses. Be aware of great opportunities for partnerships, creativity, and new projects of all kinds. Today is a good day to listen to the voice of intuition, spend time with friends and share your feelings. You might find yourself needing to remind yourself to stay on track and guard against procrastination or the desire to indulge yourself too much, or skip important steps in your work. This is not a good day to attempt resolution of conflicts with those you perceive as authority figures but it is an excellent day to write your thoughts in such matters down and to psychically ask for abundance and justice in your life. Get extra sleep tonight and be aware of your dreams as they may be prophetic.

***Meditation:*** There are many interpretations to the Moon card. One of its most interesting aspects is the conflicting interpretations of this card in Old School Tarot vs. New School Tarot. While these distinctions of Tarot Schools are greatly oversimplified, it is interesting to note that those who follow Kabbalah based schools of thought usually consider the Moon a card that indicates deception, while some of the intuitive and feminist schools of Tarot see the card as one of intuition, blessings, and abundance. To me the card is a mixture of endings and beginnings, expansion and introspection.

The Moon card obviously has much symbolism representing the unconscious and the intuition, with a pond in the foreground and animals/creatures rising out of its edge. (The creatures in the Waite based decks are often a wolf a dog and a crab/crayfish or scorpion, depending on the artist and your interpretation of the art.) In addition, the Full Moon shines down on the picture and in many Waite versions there are droplets of light falling from the Moon towards the ground/water. The pond feeds into a river that leads to the background and seems to flow right up to the mountains and on to the Moon itself. In many decks, there is a path inviting us to follow. Obviously, there is much here about connection with nature and with the instinctual and primal part of ourselves.

There are also two towers that the water runs between. The two towers are somehow different than the other images in the card, reminding us of structure and authority and of the things we build. They seem to be silent reminders of the results of our efforts and also of the consequence of our actions. The towers are a reminder of the two pillars the surround the High Priestess and are also an echo of the Tower that is depicted as being destroyed in card 16. The two towers together with the water between them suggest a gateway, perhaps a sense of buffering or protection. It seems as if we must pass between the towers and be careful to walk the middle path lest these towers ban us, or crumble as the one farther back in the journey did.

It also seems that the Towers are there to define the path and to help us orient and ground ourselves lest we become lost in the flowing waters of emotion and intuition. A few years back, on the 4$^{th}$ of July, I had this card come to life on my own property. We had a small gathering, and given our rural location, we were able to shoot fireworks. It was a full moon that evening, and while setting off a string of fireworks, the sky had the appearance of the rain/tears in the air in front of the moon. We happen to have two white pillars marking the entrance of our home, and with the glow of the moon and the fireworks, one pillar was illuminated and the other was not. In the driveway, which is directly in the center of the pillars down a long straight driveway, was, believe it or not, a crayfish, a very unusual find in Kansas to say the least. It wasn't until seeing the crayfish did it hit me that the Tarot card came to life right on my property, and I had several witnesses with me who also have Tarot knowledge to verify what I was seeing. I interpreted from this sign that I needed to draw upon all the prior lessons I've encountered and have faith that all will work out as it should during the darker moments when clarity is limited. It taught me that I was no longer operating on faith, but knowledge that I have gained from my own experience, and I needed to trust my intuition to guide me to where I needed to go next. When you study the Tableau, you will see that the two cards directly above the Moon are Justice and the Emperor. These cards are clearly indicating a theme of balance and deliberation. Yet the Moon remains a wild and mysterious card with watery and primal energy. To me this is part of the fun of the Moon. She is clearly about the abundance and joy of unbridled inspiration and a reminder not to deceive ourselves or lose touch with our day-to-day responsibilities and goals. These of course are only my thoughts and experience of this card. What are yours?

# Sun

***Predictive Meaning:*** Today is a day to stop focusing on the problems, insecurities, and spiritual challenges, and start focusing on the actions of things. Much more has been learned than you might think and so the question becomes "what are you going to do with it?" You realize that the lights are on, the burdens lifted, and you can see clearly now what might have been a mystery in the past. The pieces are connecting, and you are free, enlightened, and joyful. There are numerous blessings and help on the way, so be prepared to welcome them into your life. Focus on your own strength and try to see old information and "tried and true" ways of doing things in a new light. Also take time to play. In short, do your errands. Get to work on your part of cleaning up any old business. Then take some time to play, knowing that the Universe will provide everything you need through your own efforts and the unexpected help of spirit.

***Meditation***: A youth on a white horse rides on a sunny day with a flag of victory. Clearly this is a reminder that ultimately things do work out in life. Can you accept that? One of the spiritual challenges that the Sun card presents us with is the invitation to do a fearless self inventory and see where we really are on the journey. It is echoed by the Hierophant and the Hanged Man. This is a wonderful invitation to allow us to examine where in our life we need to rely on traditional truths, where we need a totally new perspective, and where (as represented by the Sun) it is more important to get out there and experience life than to try too hard for either approach. The Sun also comes after the sequence begun in the Hanged Man of serious spiritual initiation and trial. The Fool has grappled with the Hanged Man, Death, Temperance, the Devil, the Tower, the Star and the Moon, but why? What is the point of spiritual enlightenment if we cannot and do not bring our light into the world we live in? And if that is the message of the Sun- to bring our light into the world we live in, exactly how do we do that? How will you?

# Judgment

***Predictive Meaning:*** This is definitely a day to come out of your shell and to consider all types of new beginnings. This is particularly a good time to focus on spiritual as well as physical projects and regular world concerns. You may have felt that your physical world and spiritual world were very separate, but you will see today is a great day for bringing the two together. Luck may change for the better and new messages or information will likely come your way. Spend time with loved ones and if you feel that you are at a crossroads in your life, try not to worry over your choice. Instead listen to your instinct and watch carefully for "signs" in the physical world around you that might point you in the right direction. Today is a day to work at not being too hard on yourself or others, but also at seeing situations clearly and using good discernment. You have learned your lessons and are now renewed, refreshed, and spiritually awakened to action. You will realize that you have always been walking the spiritual path, and that every single event that occurred, from the positive ones to the challenges, were all part of the learning journey.

***Meditation:*** Echoed by Death and the Lovers, this is definitely a card that speaks of major transformations and new beginnings. The card itself looks rather like a scene out of Revelations in the Waite-Smith decks with an Angel blowing a trumpet as figures rise out of coffins that are apparently floating on water. This card definitely seems to be reminding us again and again that there are times in life when we are awakened to the fact that things are not always as they seem to be. It is time for us to look at ourselves and our world with new eyes. Questions you may want to ask yourself today include, "what Death have I been through recently and how has that shown me a new side of myself?" "How accurately am I judging and how willingly am I forgiving myself and others?" "What passion in me is re-awakening, and what is my personal Truth?"

# The World

***Predictive Meaning:*** After challenge and growth and some difficult energy to deal with, today brings us the opportunity to relax and learn through joy. Today is an important day to get things done and take care of business, but you will find that tasks you have been slogging away at for awhile are easier, and for many people certain ongoing projects will come to a satisfactory completion. Today is also a great day for health, physical activity, and responsible pleasure. You have completed the cycle; you are where you were meant to be. All the lessons on your path have been successfully achieved, and mastery awaits.

***Meditation:*** The World card comes at the end of the journey of The Fool and is in many ways a card of completion. It is also a card of beginnings as life is a circle that is endless. The card offers us rich symbolism, but also a sense of peace and beauty. One of the clearest symbols in the card is the central character of a naked woman, dancing and holding two batons. She has a scarf artfully draped across her so that we do not see her genitalia although her breasts are clearly exposed. Some schools of Tarot contend that this is because "she" is actually a hermaphrodite and that the card thus symbolizes the perfect union of male and female. I personally do not think that Hermaphrodites happen enough in nature to represent an ideal balance, but rather believe the card speaks of balancing the male/female polarity. The animals positioned around her on the four corners of the card are masculine and represent a strong and vital physical energy. They are: (in most decks) The Bull, The Lion, The Eagle and The Man.

There is also another strong lesson I see in the symbols of this card, and that is of rest and rebirth. The echo cards are the Chariot and Temperance, both strong on duality and balance, but also are cards that invite us to move to a deeper level, to the next phase in things. This too is what the World does, but her next level is the Fool once again and a continuation of the journey we have already experienced.

The card directly before her is Judgment and the one after her is The Fool. She seems to be saying that we have come through the last Judgment or the last re-thinking of our position in the world (pun intended) and are ready for some play before we start off as the Fool again on the journey. It is clearly a card of the physical world or Malkuth to the Kabbalists. What do you think?

## Exercise 12A- Developing Your Own Predictions and Meditations

In this exercise, I would like for you to pull a card and really pull out all the skills you have learned thus far in interpreting the card you select. What card was it? What is your interpretation?

_____
_____
_____
_____
_____
_____
_____
_____
_____
_____
_____
_____
_____
_____
_____

# Lesson Thirteen
# Mastering the Art of Tarot Reading

- The Structure of a Reading
- Forming Questions
- Working with Multiple Cards
- Exercise 13A- Reading Card Spreads In a New Way
- How to Determine Timing, Location, and Direction
- Understanding the Significance of Reversed Major Arcana

# The Structure of a Reading

Whenever reading Tarot or doing any spiritual work for yourself or another person you should always follow some simple spiritual steps designed to protect you as a reader and to enhance your effectiveness. Below is a basic outline of these steps, and they are presented for the sake of clarity as though you are an experienced consultant reading for another person. However, a novice doing a one-card meditation for herself should use the same steps. Many of these steps have already been outlined in the lessons; a few, such as step four, will be gone into in further detail in future lessons. For now, think of step four as the particular exercise or meditation you are doing in any given reading (as assigned at the end of each lesson). Later you can adjust this step to fit whatever method of reading you are using. Practice each of these steps until you feel totally confident in them as they form the core discipline of healthy and effective spiritual Tarot reading. These basic disciplines or steps are:

1) ***Mental Preparation***. Make sure you are clear of mind (free of alcohol, drugs, or any mind-altering substances), have plenty of time, and are well rested and not distracted. Make sure you know why you are doing the reading you are doing. Make sure the energy between you and your client is respectful and well-balanced. Get a firm and clear statement of intent that your client is open and willing for you to do the reading. Never read without permission. Take a moment to consider any possible unspoken agendas or ulterior motives either you or your client may have and clear these issues up if needed. Make sure that you and your client both are willing, for a space of time, to believe in and open yourself up to Divine insight and that you are both willing to believe that the reading will be highly successful. Also, be sure to give up any co-dependant thoughts of saving, helping, rescuing, teaching, or otherwise altering another's path. Your only expectation should be to do the best reading you can do and communicate clear information. How your advice is followed or even if it is followed is not under your control or any of your business. Those are issues of personal soul growth that only your client has the privilege to explore. Ground and center yourself to the here and now and the practical world.

2) ***Set Sacred Space.*** Psychically and physically clean the space you will be working in, and set a clear psychic and mental boundary that what you are about to do will not be interrupted by energies which are not

for the highest good of all. This should include making sure that there will be no physical interruptions. Alter the space you are in, by whatever means needed, to make it feel sacred to you. Allow for your sense of the Divine to fill the space you are in.

3) ***Attunement and Invocation.*** Take a moment to fully feel the presence of the Divine in the room and in yourself. Focus on your center or core self and allow that self to connect with the Divine. Ask for help and guidance from the Divine as you understand it and formally set your ego aside. Feel your core merging with the core of what is sacred and allow yourself to be the conduit for that energy. After gaining this sense for yourself, in a mental prayer ask for permission to do the same for your client. Then imagine your client entering a similar state to the one you are experiencing. Finally, imagine a connection of energy between you and your client. If you are doing the reading for yourself take a moment to strengthen your connection to your deepest core self.

4) ***Formulation.*** Clarify the objectives and questions to be covered in the reading. Establish a firm focus and an organized method of working through the information that will be presented. Choose which spread you will be using. Allow your client (if they so desire) to establish with you any background information that will be necessary for the reading. Through the initial reading process discover what information is known and what information makes up the key points that will be worked with to create the doorway for transformation within the reading. Then focus the reading clearly on those points of potential transformation.

5) ***Inspiration***. Allow yourself to spiritually ask for and receive inspiration, and consciously look for information and interpretations beyond what you think the cards mean or have known them to mean in the past. Pay attention to subtle details, such as cards falling out of the deck, slips of the tongue, and other unexpected indications of Spirit.

6) ***Release.*** Take a moment to consciously see your client as a living expression of Divine will. Mentally honor your client and the things you have learned from doing this reading, then sum up what you have said, re-focusing on both the positive options you found in the reading and any specific actions your client can take to bring the best results about. (If you are reading for yourself this is your Journal work.) Mentally say a prayer of thanks and allow the energy to release from

the reading with a sense of gratitude and that the best result will come as a result of the reading. Remind yourself that you cannot remain connected to the client or to how they use or perceive the reading. This is also true if the client is you. Psychically see yourself disconnecting from the reading and returning any energy the client may have sent you back to the client and reclaiming any excess energy you may have sent out.

7) ***Actions in Accord.*** Give your client or yourself any last information they may need to take the power of the reading into their own lives. Think of names of books, recommendations of specific healers, suggestions for practical actions etc. Affirm that the reading is done, congratulate the client for taking the self-nurturing step of getting the reading, and encourage him or her to use this reading in their own lives however they see fit.

8) ***Completion.*** Make sure that you take care of business and complete any energy exchange that was part of the initial reading agreement. (For example: take payment, set dates for trade, thank them for letting you practice and learn with them, whatever you need to do to complete the "contract.") Allow your client to leave the space. If you are doing the reading for yourself, allow your deep self to settle for a moment and focus with a new approach. Make note of anything that happened in this reading that was a message for you as a reader as well as a message for the client. Then take a moment to offer any final prayers and release any final energy.

9) ***Ground and center yourself.*** Re-affirm your connection with the mundane world. You can take a moment to closely observe your surroundings, have a light snack, or take a few deep breaths. Release your sense of communion with all and return to your sense of focusing only on yourself, close or complete your sacred space however you do that, and then set your plans to do something totally mundane. When you completely switch your focus back to daily life, then the reading is done.

# Forming Questions

What and how you ask the Tarot is every bit as important as how you interpret the answers. The art of asking for Divine guidance through Tarot should be thought of as sacred as prayer. It is not something to approach on a whim or in a joking manner. After all, the word divination means to communicate with the Divine. However, do not worry about getting it right at first. It may take you some time to develop your own style and sense of how to use the power of a good question. Be gentle with yourself. In the meantime, here are some pointers:

1) *Always respect free will*. This means you cannot read for another without permission. Make sure that you are not wording your questions in such a way that they are infringing on another's psychic space. For example, it is fine to ask "What do I need to know about my relationship with Fred?" or "How can I better understand Fred?" However, it is not okay to ask, "What is Fred thinking?" or "Does Fred love me or Mary more?" Respect free will and ask only what you need to know for your own growth. As a reader for other people it is important to help them see the fine lines around these types of situations and to refine their questions as needed.

2) *Don't ask the Tarot what the client already knows.* It is amazing how many people ask questions of the Tarot that they could answer with a few minutes of contemplation without the Tarot or that they already know in the present. This is ineffective for the client, as it can diminish his or her problem-solving abilities, but more important, it can also lead to "reader dependency", thus expecting you to be the one to make decisions for them. At the very least it will waste everyone's time and create a scenario where you are attracting the wrong clients. My personal take on this is that there is real and sacred power in the Tarot and it does not like to be taken for granted or diminished. Take the time to dissect the problem at hand and focus on exactly what parts of the question the client knows and which parts are confusing or unclear. This will lead to more powerful questions and thus more powerful answers.

3) *Word your question in such a way that it invites pro-active solutions and insight*. Also avoid yes/no questions as they seriously shortchange the spiritual and psychic potential of the reading. "Will I get into medical school?" is an example of a question that is a set up for a bad reading. Either the answer is yes, in which case you have not laid any

ground work to go further and learn more from the reading, or no, in which case the focus is on the negative without much room to learn what better opportunities are available instead.

4) ***Remember free will and spiritual growth are the point of all Tarot readings***. There is an age-old debate between "spiritual advisors" who consult Tarot and "fortune tellers" who abuse it. To me the difference can be summed up by imagining a client who is getting a reading about traveling.

   One reader might tell a client, "you are going to be hit by a train tomorrow." That is considered "fortune telling" and fills the client with fear. In fact, it is now possible that the client will be so upset that in an effort to avoid trains actually inadvertently put themselves in the way of one. This is what is known as a "self-fulfilling prophecy."

   On the other hand, a different reader might say, "I see that it would be far better for you to travel by car or boat, as trains seem to be a very poor choice for you tomorrow." This is sometimes considered a "spiritual counseling" response. The difference in these responses stems directly from the types of questions and expectations that form the basis for the reading. It is best to ask questions that focus on what the client can learn or do, but to also recognize the potential for outside influence. There is nothing wrong with "predictions" that enhance freedom of choice ("trains would be a dangerous choice") as external events are often the catalyst for deeper learning about ourselves and our potentials. An example of a spiritual counseling question would be "What can I do to ensure that my trip runs smoothly and I gain what I need from it?" or "What are the spiritual lessons I will encounter on this trip and how can I best prepare to embrace them?" A fortuneteller might ask, "What is the fate of this trip?" Can you see the difference? Which reader would you prefer to consult with?

5) ***Remember the squirm factor.*** Anyone who has done deep introspection and personal exploration will know that there are certain questions, that when asked of us, make us squirm. Not a negative, fearful squirm which is our intuition telling us to back off, but an uncomfortable, yet compelling squirm that is our intuition telling us that our ego may be challenged and true growth is about to happen. These are the questions that hold some essential grain of truth and spiritual promise.

There is no formula for knowing how to find these questions. They elicit a kind of awe and fear and faith in great things all rolled into one. The key is to learn to recognize this squirm for what it is when we come across it in others or ourselves and to jump on the opportunity. When you encounter questions like these in yourself, write them down and do a Tarot reading on them as soon as possible. When you encounter them in your clients, trust them for what they are and enter into the reading with enthusiasm. In any case, every time you encounter these questions feel blessed. You are about to partake of the great work and the great blessing of Tarot: true self-transformation.

## Working with Multiple Cards and Simple Spreads

One of the hardest aspects of reading the Tarot is making the jump from interpreting a single card to interpreting cards in groups or spreads. This is first and foremost because most of us learn to think of cards in terms of having "meanings" and correct interpretations instead of learning to deeply and carefully look at the spread as a story, with each individual card serving as a chapter or page of that story.

A terrific way to get around this tendency is to completely change the process that you think of as "reading the cards." When working with multiple cards try not to work with individual meanings or even individual cards. Instead try to look for the following factors:

1) ***Notice what cards are there and what ones are not.*** Are there more cards of one suit there than another? Are Court cards represented? How many Major Arcana? How balanced are the representations of the different kinds of cards? Do you have many more of one type than another? How many cards with the same number appear? Are there no Kings, no Aces, etc?

    A little contemplation will show you quickly that a three-card spread with two Court cards in it has a very different meaning than a three-card spread with all numbered Minor Arcana. The same is true of a 3-card spread with two or more Major Arcana, or spreads that have too many or two few of any particular suit.

2) ***Notice sequencing.*** Do you have three courts but not the fourth? That is quite significant. Do you have a 7 and a 9 of the same suit but not the 8? How about Major Arcana? Do you have three cards from the Journey of the Fool in order? Do you have cards from the Major

Arcana that fall into columns (echo cards)? Or do you have a run of cards that go in sequence but a card is missing? Look for and notice these details. They can be huge clues.

3) ***Check the balance of "elements" in your spread.*** Do you have lots of cups, as well as Major Arcana cards that seem "watery" to you? Do you have lots of fiery cards? This can have an impact on the overall meaning of the spread. For example: lots of fire might indicate passions are high and change will be rapid. Lots of earth might mean that things will happen more slowly and grow over time and bear fruit in the right season. The emotional tone of the client, and the emotional tone of how you want to deliver your message, will also likely be different depending on what element or elements are prominent in a reading.

4) ***Look for the card that stands out as different from the rest.*** Do you have all Major Arcana and only one Minor Arcana, or visa versa? Is there a single Ace or a single Court card? Think in terms of the structure of the deck as well as in terms of the meanings of individual cards themselves, and you will get helpful clues. Also, remember that not every card in every reading has equal weight. A Tarot reading is rather like a sentence, every word or card needs to be there, but some of them are there to convey the central message and some of them are just there to connect things together. For example, you go to a restaurant and order a burger and fries, and you get a burger on your plate, and also get fries on your plate but you don't get "and" on your plate. Cards are like that too. By looking for the cards that are alike, those that are different, and those which stand out, you will start to get an intuitive feeling for which cards in a reading deserve the bulk of your time and attention and which ones are merely "helper" or clarifying cards.

# Exercise 13A: Reading the Clues in Spreads Based on the Structure of the Deck

This exercise shows you how to do some readings without the cards. As strange as it seems, try to discover what you already know about these readings without getting these cards out of your deck and meditating on the pictures and without referring to what you think the cards mean. The goal here is to train yourself to think in terms of combinations of cards and how they relate to the overall structure of the deck. Use what you know about the structure of the Tarot, and about the overall characteristics of the different suits and types of cards. Meditate on what you think the types of groupings might mean in the five examples given below.

Assume that you are doing a three-card spread on the question "What do I most need to know for my spiritual growth at this time?" where all three cards are without specific position meanings. What would you notice? As always, do the entire reading process, including setting sacred space and writing the answers down in your Journal. Remember you can write down insights and answers as well as questions that might spring to mind that could only be answered with more information. This exercise should in fact leave you with questions that could only be answered by further examination of the actual cards.

Reading One: Three Sword cards (no courts)

Reading Two: Two Queens and the Empress

Reading Three: Priestess, Hermit, Tower

Reading Four: Fool and two Wand cards

Reading Five: Knight of Cups, Page of Wands, Magician

## Example of Reading the Clues in Spreads Based on the Structure of the Deck

### *A Cup, a Pentacle, and a Wand Card*

The first thing that I notice is that there are no Major Arcana and no Sword cards. I would say that the issue is not a big spiritual lesson (Majors) and it is not something that the client is approaching from an intellectual place either (Swords.) This is fascinating considering the question was "What do I need to know for my spiritual growth at this time?" My first answer might be, "not much, it is what you do about your practical world that matters most right now." It seems to me that this is a day-to-day issue and that what is required is a fairly balanced approach (three out of four Minors.) Because the Cup card means emotions to me and the Wand card I interpret to indicate passion as well as hands on experience, I would say that the client might be emotionally keyed up and really needing the patience that the Pentacle card might be offering.

I would take these first impressions and then look at the actual card meanings and symbols on the cards to look for practical daily actions the client can take. I would be particularly interested to see what type of grounding or stability the Pentacle card could lead us to finding.

## Determining the "When and the Where" in a Reading

As stated previously, the difference between an ordinary consultant and an expert is mastery of the Tarot language. Being able to uncover the "when" and the "where" of the events discussed in a reading is of major benefit. My method of determining timing and/or location is actually quite simple to do, but is extremely accurate. In fact, it's the main reason why my clients are willing to wait days for an appointment with me when there are readers available literally across the street, open and available for walk in clients. My clients are convinced that I am a psychic extraordinaire. Hardly so! Some think I am able to pull details from thin air. To some extent I am. I simply have mastered the art of the Tarot timetable. Now you can too.

Let's say you do a multi card spread for an individual who has come for help in deciding which of two job offers she should take. Both are equal in pay and she believes she would have the same growth potential with both as well. In fact, they are so similar she simply cannot figure out which of the two offers to take, and obviously she cannot say yes to both. Perhaps she is torn because neither are truly the right one, and she should continue her search. She is hoping the Tarot will offer her the insight she does not have at this time to make the best decision for her.

When you are done with the reading, after you have drawn all the cards and discussed the substance of each one in the spread, examine the preponderance of suits. Depending on the spread you use, the suit that dominates determines the location of the job she should accept. If you are using any spread that has at least 10 cards or 10 positions, such as the Celtic Cross or the Astrological wheel, then cards 6 and 10 in that spread, in addition to whatever their position meaning is, will indicate direction and location. For smaller spreads, it will be the predominance of the suit. For example, let's say that the Cups were the dominant suit in a five-card spread. This would indicate her best choice is the job that is the most west of her current location, or in this case her former job, is the one indicated.

Timing is another detail that my clients really want to know. Many times, an individual knows "the what" and "the how" already, but they want to know when an event like a promotion or marriage proposal will occur. Just as the suits determine location, they can determine timing as well. Refer to the following chart. Practice and memorize it, and you will see that this small amount of information will add significant depth and insight to your readings.

## Determining Timing and Location

| *If the Predominant Suit is* | *then timing is this long* | *and the direction is* |
|---|---|---|
| Major Arcana | now or at any time | current location |
| Wands | number on card in days | South |
| Cups | number on card in weeks | West |
| Swords | number on card in months | East |
| Pentacles | number on card in years* | North |

*Pentacles can also indicate cycles, seasons, or already determined lengths of time such as contracts, leases, semesters of study, etc.

Let's refer again to my client's reading about her job situation. Mindy also wants to know when she will actually start this job, as no definite time was indicated by either employer. There are several ways to find dates, depending on the spread you are using. If you use a multi-card spread such as the Celtic or Double Celtic Cross, then card 4 has been used to determine timing, in addition to its already existing meaning in the spread. If not using a very large spread, you will need to choose one that has at least four cards to determine timing. Otherwise, you will need to pull one card when you are done with the reading specifically with the intention of indicating timing.

In Mindy's reading, the two of cups appeared. Therefore, consulting the chart provided before, she will encounter or start this job within two weeks.

## Understanding the Significance of Reversed Major Arcana

In chapter 8, we discussed the necessity of utilizing reversed cards in a reading, and not just turning them upright or ignoring their appearance. Every card, whether upright or reversed, offers significance in appearing just as it is. The Major Arcana cards are no exception. We discussed earlier that Major Arcana cards indicate spiritual lessons and major learning events. So, what do reversed Major Arcana represent?

In addition to the numerous options offered in chapter 8, reversed Major Arcana hold a unique purpose in the Tarot. While it's been stated in many books that they represent a diminished presence of the card (Empress Reversed might indicate a lack of fully manifested creativity or abundance), no one has really explained the higher importance of a reversed Major Arcana card until now. You are already familiar with the journey of the Fool representing the journey of life's spiritual lessons, starting as the Fool and achieving completion and mastery with the World. Have you ever wondered what happened to the Fool after the World?

Most books leave you thinking it's all "happily ever after" from there, but that is simply not the case. When the Fool finally reaches the World, he has in fact mastered his lessons the first time around. However, there is a difference between someone who has mastered the study of a lesson and someone who can apply those lessons to daily life. Reversed Major Arcana cards indicate that this is a lesson that requires application and hands on experience. They tell us its time to "walk the walk" and live by example, serving as a teacher of the lesson itself. The client therefore is the character of the card itself. If the reversed High Priestess appears, this indicates that the client is the High Priestess, currently holding the ability to offer insight to herself and others. However, because this is a new role for your client, she is unaware of her ability. It is the reader's responsibility to explain this in detail to the client, and help bring this ability to their attention.

Another scenario with Reversed Major Arcana is that your clients are likely in the midst of obstacles that they are quite discouraged about. They are tired, angry, and frustrated because he or she thought this situation was already dealt with in the past. And this is in fact the case. Also, reversed Major Arcana lessons are often deeper in intensity that upright Major Arcana lessons, which add additional burden to the client. Usually the client is unaware of why all of this is happening again. "If I already confronted my inner demons in regards to my addiction" a woman once declared during her reading, "then why is the same situation back with a vengeance?" To answer her question, this happens in order to motivate her to rise to the occasion, demonstrate her newly found skills, and to show this to others as well as herself. There is a difference between simply reading a book and knowing its contents inside and out. As such, reversed Major Arcana challenge us to dig into the depths of ourselves and propel us further along on our spiritual path. Its time to review the lessons we mastered on the journey and put them to use.

Therefore, when you do a reading for a client (or yourself) and you see several reversed Major Arcana in the reading, congratulate them on their previous success with those lessons. It is your job now to help them understand that now is the time for them to expect to teach a Fool in their own life, someone who will draw inspiration and wisdom from their stories and experiences from their own personal journey. Since we go though life continually growing and encountering more and more advanced lessons, the journey of the Fool is not a one-time event but an ever-existing wheel of opportunity.

# Lesson Fourteen
# Working with Spreads

- Understanding What a Spread Really Is
- Choosing and Using Spreads
- Discovering the Secrets of Line and Pattern within a Spread
- Exercise 14A: Creating Your Own Spread
- Example Spread: The Financial Abundance Spread
- Example Spread: The Romantic Relationship Spread
- Sample Reading Interpreting the Relationship Spread
- Exercise 14B: Practice Using the Relationship Spread
- Working with Larger Spreads: The Celtic Cross and Double Celtic Cross

# Understanding What a Spread Really Is

A Tarot spread is simply a group of Tarot cards laid out in particular pattern with a special meaning assigned to each card in the pattern. You can think of the cards as answers to specific questions that the positions in the pattern are asking. You can think of the whole pattern like a dot-to-dot drawing that is asking an overall question. So, for example, the overall question might be "Should I marry Joe?" and the "answer" might be in a card (or spread) that deals with relationships. That overall answer would involve many smaller answers to questions such as "Do we really have that much in common?" and "Are we communicating effectively?" The smaller answers would come in the form of points in the pattern that are marked by individual cards. By interpreting the cards to find all the smaller answers you can then synthesize your information to answer the overall question. Looking for all the specifics and pulling them together into an overall message is the process of reading a Tarot spread.

# Choosing and Using Spreads

Many new students of Tarot (and many old ones too) try to learn as many different spreads as they possibly can, thinking this will make them a more effective reader. I don't recommend this approach as it rarely gains results anywhere near comparable to the effort it takes. Instead, I recommend that you work with fewer spreads and work with them more deeply. In my professional practice, I almost always use the same spread and if the need arises I will ask the client to pull a few additional cards at the very end for further clarity.

I have similar feelings regarding how large a spread should be. While there are spreads out there that take 30 or 40 cards, or even the whole deck, there seems to be little point in putting out so many that the randomness is gone. In theory using most of all of the deck diminishes the Divine aspects of divination, as of course, every card is going to show up at some point or another. Plus, to completely interpret all those cards could take hours. As humans, we simply cannot absorb and use that much information at one time so it would be very overwhelming to the average client.

This is the real secret of using Tarot spreads to their fullest, and a well-kept secret at that. Learn what the spread itself symbolizes and learn how the different energies within the spread are meant to interact. Then take these factors into account when interpreting individual cards and the spread as a unit. Even one card, if interpreted correctly, can be a very powerful spread in itself.

Often spreads will indicate a series of steps. Really understanding these cards as a unit can start to tell you a great deal about which cards are just space fillers. (For example: you need to do that step but you already know it and there is no significantly new information there) and which ones are there to point out to you new and useful perspectives on things. (For example, a card that seems to scream "look out" this is a step you cannot afford to ignore or gloss over.)

## Discovering the Secrets of Line and Pattern within a Spread

How do you learn these things about spreads? Some spread authors will tell you when they explain the spread. There is an example of this at the end of this lesson. More often than not, however, they don't provide this information. In this case you simply need to throw your logical mind out the window, stop worrying about being right, and play around. Your intuition will start suggesting patterns within the patterns and implied relationships between certain points in the spread. That is why I have not featured any commonly known spreads. There are numerous books available as well as resources online that offer literally hundreds of spread options. Until you understand how a spread works, utilizing a spread someone else created will not help you develop your own intuition and insight. It might not even work for you. But don't get discouraged.

The concept of how a spread is put together can seem fairly confusing at first. However, it becomes clear once you try to do it yourself. For this reason, every reader should invent one or two spreads of their own, even if they choose not to read with them and instead use a standard spread they have learned from others. Plus, it is a great idea to prepare to be spontaneous should a client request a reading on a subject matter that doesn't conform to a traditional spread.

## Exercise 14A: Creating Your Own Spread

Think of a question you might ask in a reading, such as "Will I get this new job?" or "Should I date Frank?" then think of a very simple picture (stick drawing) you could create to symbolize your question. For example, you might choose a doorway for the new job (getting your foot in the door) or a heart shape for dating. Draw it out in very simple 5-year-old stick figure style. Then draw a "dot" where lines intersect or in the middle of long lines. Now erase the lines, leaving you with the dots. This is all there is to creating a spread. All you have to do is imagine what the different parts of the drawing might symbolize and then assign a card number and meaning to each one. What are your ideas for spreads? Jot down your ideas below.

# Sample Spreads

***Financial Abundance Spread.*** This spread looks like a torso and its two arms.

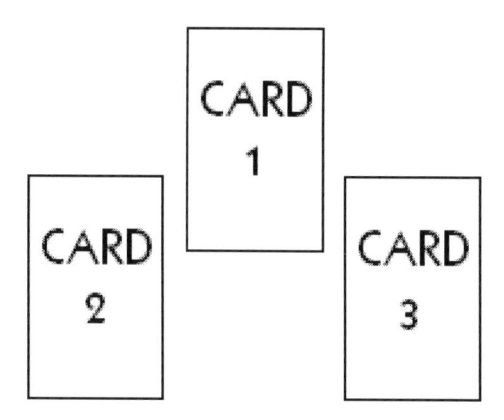

```
        CARD
         1
CARD          CARD
 2             3
```

1) ***The head and heart.*** This is how the person is seeing himself and how they perceive the situation. This card will also indicate how capable the person is at the moment to make changes in their situation. Remember that although we can all create the lives we want to live and change is always possible, the person has to be ready to take their power and embrace change. This card will let you know if the person needs more rest and healing or if they are currently ready to go out there and conquer the world.

2) ***The left hand.*** (Read the cards left to right as they relate to you, not the client- as the information is being given to you to interpret so it will arrange itself around your experience.) This indicates how clear the person is about what they really want. It also shows how open to spiritual guidance the client is right now in regards to financial abundance. This card is the major indicator of opportunities that may be available to the client and how well they are accepting and integrating those opportunities.

3) ***The right hand.*** This card is all about action. Is the client willing to take action? Are the actions being taken appropriate ones? This card is also where the ability to sustain action and follow through with good common sense will be indicated. It is also a position that will tell you about how the emotional effects of the situation are being played out in the life of the client. Future opportunities that are brought on by taking specific, concrete actions can also be seen in this position.

***Romantic Relationship Spread***. This spread is designed to look like a cup or vessel.

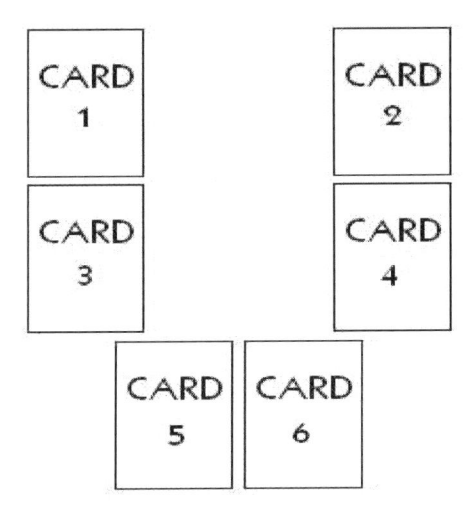

```
CARD        CARD
  1           2

CARD        CARD
  3           4

      CARD CARD
        5    6
```

1) ***Attraction***: What draws these people together (or not)? What does one think the other will bring them?

2) ***Affinity:*** What do the two people truly have in common and what (other than physical attraction) is it that can draw them together? Where are they alike and comfortable with each other?

3) ***Communication***: How well do the people involved really communicate and understand one another? Do the messages they think they are getting have anything to do with the messages the other person thinks they are sending?

4) ***Respect***: How much true respect is there here? Are they willing to have the other person truly be different, or are they hoping to change the other person?

5) ***Conflict:*** Do they know how to fight well and fairly? Is there a potential for emotional or physical violence? Are they both equally interested in growing and learning and changing as part of the relationship, or is attention focused on one of the two as the main source of the problem?

6) ***Bonding and Outcome:*** What are the potential probabilities of this relationship? Is there a deeper soul lesson here or is it just personality interaction?

# Sample Reading: Interpreting the Relationship Spread

The first two cards should give you a quick look at the relationship as the client is seeing it. This is what is happening on the surface and the area from which most of the questions and concerns that your client asks will come from. The two cards should be read as a pair. Look at how alike or different the two cards are in coloring, suit, mood, and theme. The more alike the cards are, the more secure the relationship will seem on the surface. The more different the cards the more things will appear to be turbulent in the relationship.

The next two cards are the really important ones. These are the "heart of the matter" cards. Although the themes and issues reflected in these cards might not be obvious at first, they are where the core of any problems and the seed to any solutions can be found. Again, look for how these cards work as a pair.

The final pair of cards serves as a "destiny" pair. This is where the spiritual lessons to be learned will be shown and where a sense of future possibility for the relationship will show. As above, read these cards as a pair. Also, read these cards as the source of messages that move up the sides of the cup. In this way, you can read a line of cause and effect in the cards on each side. Cards 5, 3, and 1 show what is pulling these two into the relationship. Cards 6, 4, and 2 show what is stabilizing the relationship and keeping both parties involved.

Side #1, Cards 5, 3 and 1: Conflict, Communication and Attraction. Remember even the most healthy of relationships are a source of healing for our own inner conflicts. We attract things to us based on what we are broadcasting energetically, so if we do not like what we are seeing, we have the opportunity to change our signal. If there is good communication this becomes a dynamic, creative, and rejuvenating force.

Side #2, Cards 6, 4, and 2: Bonding, Respect and Affinity. These are the forces that make love last. Be aware that many people confuse bonding and affinity. For example, a couple who have faced unemployment and a cross country move may be very bonded and feel that "we are in this together," but they may also have very different interests and not have much to share. They may even begin to bore each other after a while. As you can see both are needed to sustain a relationship. As with the first line, the middle card is the key. Respect is what allows us to look for interests we can share and to learn from each other, which creates a greater sense of affinity. And of course, respect is the single most necessary ingredient in bonding. The only way not to be driven crazy by the "little annoying habits" that all people have is to have a respect for them that outweighs the minor stuff. If you really think someone is a genius and remind yourself of that often, it is somehow easier to deal with the fact that she leaves her dirty socks on the floor. This is even more important in times of crisis.

After you have looked at individual cards and the cards as a pair, step back and look at the whole picture. If the relationship is strong this will look like a full cup or a solid vessel if it is not you will get a sense of it being fragile or empty. In some cases, the cards make this point quite literally by putting the pictures together so that you seem to see a leak or a break in the pattern.

## Exercise 14B: Practice Using the Relationship Spread

Here is a layout using the relationship spread. Without trying to interpret individual cards notice what you can tell about these patterns.

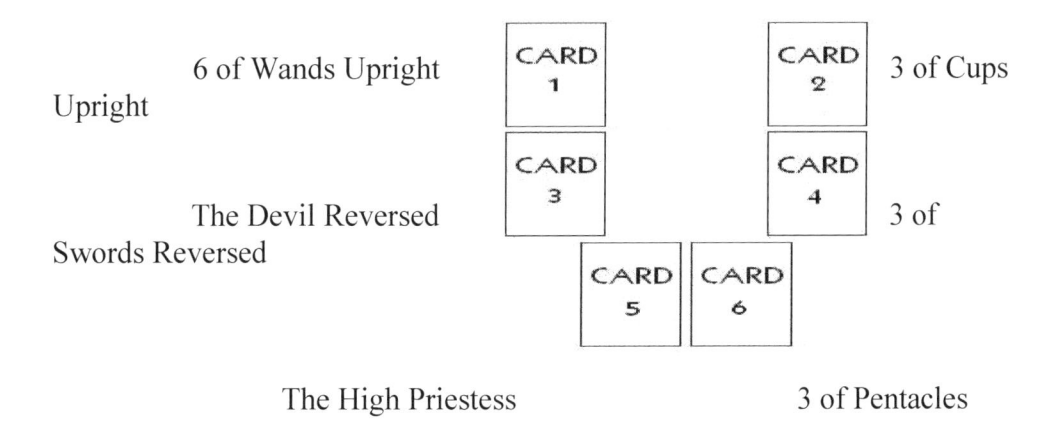

```
                    6 of Wands Upright    [CARD 1]         [CARD 2]    3 of Cups
Upright

                    The Devil Reversed    [CARD 3]         [CARD 4]    3 of
Swords Reversed
                                             [CARD 5] [CARD 6]

                    The High Priestess                            3 of Pentacles
```

**Write down your interpretation below.**

# Example: Practice Using the Relationship Spread

Without trying to interpret individual cards I notice some really striking factors. The only two reversed cards are the middle pair, which is the "heart of the matter." There is some definite conflict here, and respect and communications have been seriously compromised. The only two Major Arcana show on the side of attraction. The pull between these two people might be greater than their ability to sustain the relationship. In other words, lots of sparks, not lots of stability. I also notice that on the top level or the "shallow" level it looks good and also on the bottom level or the deepest level it looks pretty good. Maybe there is a deep spiritual connection as well as a surface attraction, but they simply have not yet learned how to do the "normal, real-world" part of the relationship. Also, the Devil is the only really dark card. When you step back and look at the cup as a whole, it looks like a drain or a leak. The rest of the cards are fairly light, even the 3 of Swords is not that dark and ominous in the Waite Smith deck (remember the deck will affect the interpretation.) The Devil is in the communication position.

Before I even try to interpret card by card I have a sense that the key here is communication and that there is a very big attraction between these people, both spiritual and mundane. As I go through and look at the cards individually I can start to look for specific information about how they can best communicate, what secrets or other wounds to communication and trust need to be brought out in the open and healed, and how they can best work together as a team in daily life. I also know because the top cards look pretty rosy (and the six of wands in the Waite deck looks quite sexual) that they may not be noticing all this stuff right now.

What did you get? You probably discovered some of the same issues and probably some very different ones as well. Don't worry. Remember that we all interpret cards differently according to our experiences.

# Working with Larger Spreads: The Celtic and Double Celtic Cross

Some readers believe that it is more complicated to read with larger spreads, as the more cards are being used, the harder it will be to make your interpretation. I too believed this when I was a student many years ago, but learned that it was (for me) quite the opposite. Once you know your personal definition of each card, you may find that having more cards in a spread help you piece together a more accurate story for your client or yourself.

Do not be intimidated by the following two spreads. How you interpret a 10 or 21 card spread is not any different than a 3 or 5 card spread. All that you need is more time available to do your consultation.

The Celtic Cross spread is one of the most common tarot spreads. There is a cross in the center, with a row of 4 cards along the side. This spread will provide a fairly in-depth look at a situation including past, present and external influences.

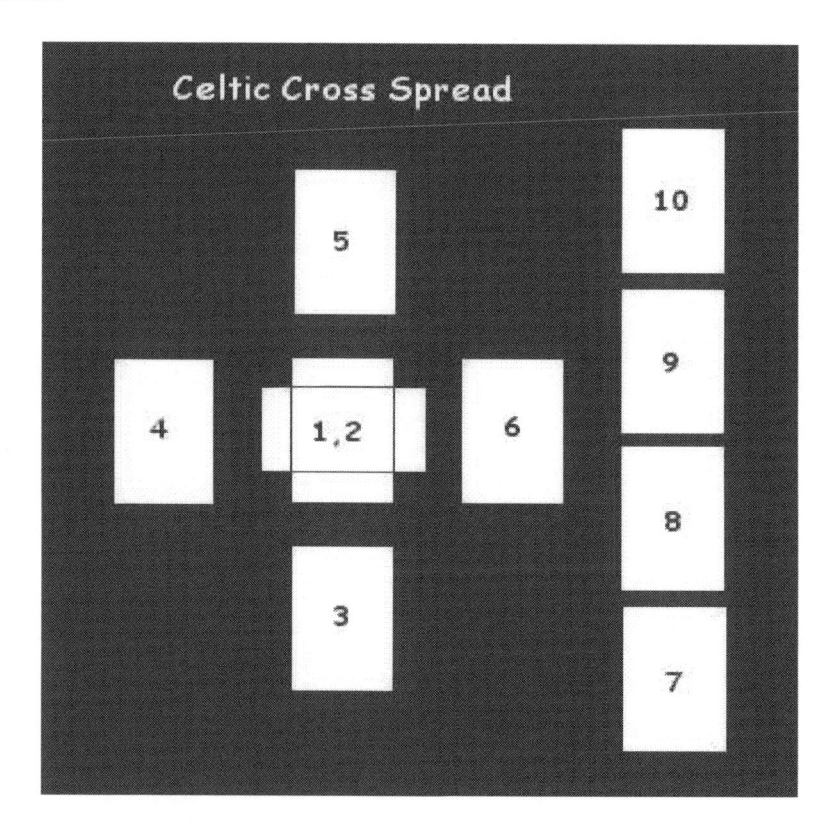

**1. The Issue**
   This is the main issue the cards will discuss in the spread.

**2. Further information on the issue**
   What the question is based on; further information about the issue at hand.

**3. Foundation of the issue**
   Details that are unconscious to the client, but affect the issue

**4. The Past**
   What past issues relate to the question, or how things used to be.

**5. Issues ready to manifest**
   What is about to happen, especially if the client did not get the reading.

**6. The near future**
   The next event that you will see regarding the issue.

**7. The destiny of the situation**
   What you can expect to happen if you continue what you are doing and do not change anything.

**8. Relationships**
   Not necessarily romantic in nature, but rather how this situation affects others and how you are dealing with them in relation to the question.

**9. Hopes and or Fears**
   Obstacles or helpful influences around you.

**10. Final Outcome**
   What the client should expect to manifest if he or she adheres to the advice of the reading.

## Double Celtic Cross

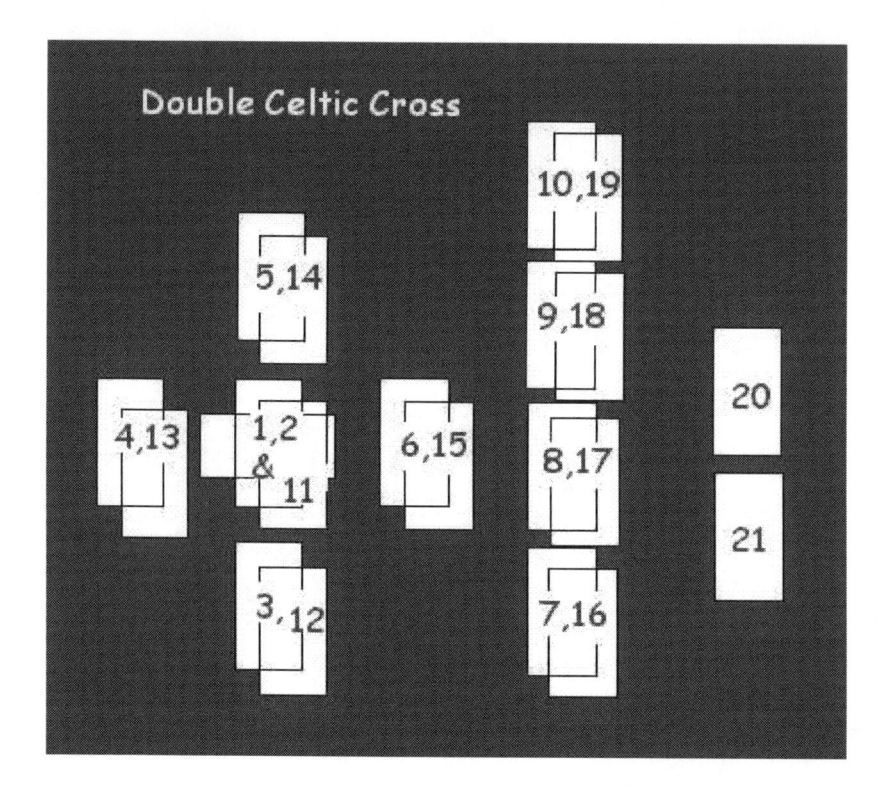

The Double Celtic Cross spread is the same as the regular Celtic Cross spread, except you add a second layer of cards to every position. View the graphic for the layout description. Since you are meant to read the cards in groups, as they are layered two deep in a single position, it is best to analyze them in order of position rather than in numerical order.

Cards 1 and 11 are read together, representing what is a description of the present situation, or what is in the mind of the client that has prompted him or her to seek your counsel.

Card 2 represents an obstacle to that situation, or a factor involved in which way it will swing. Depending on context of the surrounding cards, this can be an opposing factor or a helpful one.

Cards 3 and 12 are read next, in the position of the foundation of the matter, or the influence in the client's life which has enabled them to become the person they are today, and will show some frame of reference as to how they will handle this situation in question.

Cards 4 and 13 are read together, representing the recent phase which the client has been passing through. This will show how the situation has been presenting itself, and how the client has been dealing with it thus far.

Cards 5 and 14 are read next, and they show a public view of how the situation appears. Often giving a view to a possible outcome, these cards show one way this situation could resolve if the client continues on in the same manner as he or she is currently operating.

Cards 6 and 15 are read together in the position of the phase the client will be moving into in the coming period of time (days, weeks). They will also be an indication of how the client will deal with the situation in that time.

Cards number 7 and 16 represent the psychological level or mindset of the client in regards to the situation at hand. It may be something that the client has not wanted to deal with, or has been unaware of.

Cards number 8 and 17 are read next, representing the relationships aspect of the situation for the client. This is in regards to the other people in the client's life who are affected by this situation, and can show their perspectives as well as who the key players are.

Cards number 9 and 18 are read together, representing the client's conscious hopes and fears, or their goals and desires regarding the situation. These goals can be goals of avoidance as well as goals of achievement.

Cards number 10 and 19 are read next, these pose the Final Outcome to the client. Summing up everything else that has gone before, this would be pretty much the end result of the reading.

There are two more cards left, these are posted off to the side and represent timing and advice of the cards. The advice of the cards should be interpreted as a key action or figure in the situation that shows the client how to handle the advice given throughout the reading.

The timing is more complicated, giving the time interval covered by the spread. The suit will indicate to the reader the following:

- Rods....................days
- Cups....................weeks
- Swords.............months
- Pentacles...........years

The numbers of the cards themselves will indicate the number of days, weeks or months as follows:

- Aces through tens.....one through ten
- Pages.................eleven
- Knights..............twelve
- Queens......... .thirteen
- Kings............fourteen

Lastly, if any Major Arcana cards come up under timing at all, it indicates immediacy and that the client has already set into motion that which will determine the outcome of the situation.

Remember, Tarot is an intuitive art. I have tried to break down the intuitive process into steps that you can see, think about, and even repeat. In readings, however, it is much more of a sense of flow and discovery. Go where your gut leads you and trust yourself.

You have all the tools you need now. All you need to do now to master the art of Tarot is practice.

# Lesson Fifteen
# Final Thoughts on Reading for Yourself and Others

- Traits of a Good Reader
- Completion and Self Assessment
- Your Graduation Certificate
- About the Author

# Congratulations!

By now you have explored all you need to know in order to be able to read Tarot for yourself and others. All that is missing is experience that only practice can offer. In fact, the very best thing you can do at this point in order to truly master Tarot is to set a goal to do 100 readings. Do 50 readings for yourself and 50 readings for other people. This will give you a chance to try out what you know and begin putting all this information together to create your own reading style.

## Thoughts on Reading for Yourself and Others

- When reading for yourself, make sure you are open to a real answer. Don't fall into the trap of doing a reading over and over until you get one you like. Remember we are asking the Divine for advice and not what we want. This will simply undermine your relationship to the Tarot and make all of your readings less satisfactory. When you read for yourself, make sure you set a clear question and are open to genuinely exploring that question. Then, if you do not get an interpretation you understand or like, make sure to give yourself the gift of really thinking about it for at least 48 hours before you revise your question and do another reading on the same topic.

- When reading for yourself, make sure you take extra time to ground and set sacred space. When you read for others you are agreeing to be a clear channel for spiritual and intuitive information. When you are reading for yourself you are doing the same thing except that you are also the one receiving the information. In some cases, this is easy and in other cases this is challenging. Be sure that when you are reading for yourself you do not skip steps.

- Consider using a bias card if it is an emotionally charged reading, either for yourself or someone else. A bias card is simply a one card reading on what the question and the answer to the question is not about. You read the bias card first, before the rest of the reading and then you set it aside.

  Doing a bias reading can help you avoid the trap some readers fall into of interpreting nearly every reading the same way, and focusing on the same spiritual insights over and over again to the exclusion of all others. For example, you may have met people who have just entered 12 step programs, for whom the answer to every question is that it is about addiction. What this does over time is it reduces the power and insight when the problem really is about addiction, and causes other people to take them less seriously. It is rather like crying wolf. A bias card reading is designed to show you where you might be tempted to focus but do not need to focus today. So, if for example my question is "What do I need to do to improve my relationship with Fred?" and I get a bias card of the King of Cups which I interpret as "the ability to communicate deeply about feelings and long range goals" then I know in the reading I don't need to be looking for how to communicate better with Fred and instead I need to look at other aspects and actions that could enlighten or improve the relationship. If on the other hand I got the King of Cups not as the bias but in the main reading then maybe my interpretation would be to sit down and have a long chat with Fred about where our relationship is going.

- It may take a few tries to get a feel for bias readings but most people who work with this idea like it a lot and it can be especially valuable if you are reading for a highly charged emotional situation, or if you are a professional reader doing a great number of readings in a row.

- Remember to Have Fun. Tarot should be fun. If it is not, go bowling. No real human growth, spiritual insight, or clear information about the world around us is possible if we lose our sense of humor and play.

## Traits of a Good Tarot Reader

- They have a clear intention and are not reading out of ego traps. This means that you are reading because you are fascinated with Tarot and interested in sharing the insights you can gain through a reading. It does not mean you are trying to impress anyone, fix anyone, or taking on the responsibility for making sure the client "gets it." You can only be responsible for being a clear source of the best information you know how to give. You cannot and should not concern yourself with how other people respond to or use the information. Their growth is their business. This may seem detached, but if you talk to experienced readers about their "worst reading experiences" you will find that 99 times out of 100 things got off track when the reader allowed his or her own emotions to get in the way.

- They answer the question. Many Tarot readers talk too much about general theory and not enough about specifics. They talk about what the cards mean without relating those meanings to the questions at hand. This is why so much of this course has focused on looking at a particular symbol or aspect of a card and then creating a meaning. It is to get you used to synthesizing information. Now that you have that skill, you can synthesize the meaning of the cards with the questions being asked and create a more effective reading.

Don't make the mistake many readers make of asking the question, selecting the cards and talking about the cards but not about how the cards answer the question at hand. If you simply remind yourself to relate every observation you have back to the question you will find your readings are much more powerful and not incidentally much easier to give. Your client is not requesting a reading to hear about how you are knowledgeable about the history of the Swords, but rather what the Swords mean in relation to their question. If your client does not wish to share with you the question at hand, then remember to relate your interpretation based on the card in the spread which defines the client.

- They listen well. In order to listen to the question, you need to actually understand it. You would be surprised by how often people launch into looking for an answer in a reading when the answer they are looking for is not exactly the answer the client asked for. The remedy for this is to take your time and really listen. When you listen, don't judge your client or try to change them. Just take the time to really understand their perspectives, priorities, and concerns.

- Great readers dare to be wrong. You can too. Just say what you see in the cards and what you think they mean. Asking too many questions or speaking in vague terms until you get affirmation from the client tends to reduce their confidence and make you look like you are guessing. Speak in clear and concise language and make short firm statements based on your best sense of what you are seeing and what you think it means. If you are indeed "wrong," a strong and healthy client will be able to figure that out for themselves. In fact, it is the client's job to take what you are saying and figure out how to take what they need from the reading. It is your job to simply say what you see.

- They leave the client with new options for taking constructive action. Instead of simply saying "this is what will happen, take it or leave it," good readers look for clues in the cards of how the client can take their power and have a positive impact on their own life situations. When you read, try to look for specific, active, constructive suggestions and refrain from excessive spiritual philosophy that the client may not necessarily understand. Speak in a language the client understands. If your client is not immersed in New Age and occult philosophy, don't talk about "resonating their etheric fields to harmonize with the elemental vibrations of their chakras." Try telling them that they need to get clear about what they want. Every person on the planet talks differently, even when we think we speak the same language. Great readers really listen to not only what their clients are saying but how they are saying it so that they can establish rapport and speak in images that the client can really connect with.

- They are compassionate. Getting a reading should be a joy. If you are in a bad mood, don't like someone, or tend to want to judge your clients, refrain from reading until the situation changes. Reading should be something you enjoy doing for people you enjoy connecting with and for whom you can feel respect and compassion even (and especially) when you don't agree with them. If you can't read with compassion, refuse or reschedule the reading.

## Completion and Self-Assessment

By now you have done a great deal of work exploring the Tarot in new ways. One of the best techniques for integrating any knowledge and making it second nature is to take the time to acknowledge and celebrate it. To mark this study coming to an end, create for yourself a small graduation ceremony.

Set up sacred space and ground as usual. Then gather together your favorite art supplies (or some paper and crayons if you think you are not visually creative), your class notebook and/or Tarot Journal and complete the following exercise.

- Take a moment to pull out your Tarot journal and look at the very first card you interpreted in this lesson.

- How confident did you feel doing the exercise in lesson one?

- How much were you relying on remembering a meaning or doing things "right" and how much were you just letting things flow?

- Could you have done a reading (without a book for aid) for a friend or loved one right then?

- Could you do so now?

- How has your exploration of the material in this book helped to define or deepen your spiritual journey?

- What differences do you notice in the quality and depth of your current Tarot reading?

- What exactly have you learned about yourself and about the Tarot?

- Take a moment to think about these questions and any others that spring to mind, and journal about them. Write an acknowledgment of the work you have done and the insight you have received.

- You have taught yourself much about who you are, the spiritual path you are on, and Tarot. When you are done, display your graduation creation where you will see it and be reminded of this gift you have given yourself.

At this point you are well on your way to being an outstanding Tarot reader. All that is left now is practice and patience. In time as you work with the cards, your intuition will deepen, and soon you will be able to use your newly found knowledge and insight to read the story the Tarot tells. It is wonderful to know that the art of Tarot is growing and helping us all to go farther with our spiritual journeys.

It was my pleasure to share this experience with you. I bid you peace.

Namaste!

"Aruna" Dawn Grey

# WMA Tarot School

I, _____

Formally announce successful completion of all assignments and exercises in

# Reading the Tarot

And hereby earn this certificate of graduation

On this day

_____

# About the Author

"Aruna" Dawn Grey began her Tarot journey in 1990 when she purchased her first deck of cards at a metaphysical store near her college in NJ. After many years of independent study, she enrolled in formal training under the supervision of John Gilbert, Tarot Grandmaster and founder of the Tarot Institute. She spent the next four years immersed in full time study. In the years to come, Dawn earned the rank of Certified Tarot Master Instructor with the Tarot Certification Board of America, a status obtained by only a handful of individuals worldwide.

In 2002, she was appointed Vice President of Education of the American Tarot Association, an organization dedicated to teaching and preserving the ways of Tarot. From there Dawn developed her own Tarot course, and has since taught over 2,000 students distantly and her in local community.
She offers consultations in Tarot and other Metaphysical modalities in person, over the telephone, and via internet by appointment. For more information, email her at reikirays@yahoo.com.

Dawn is the President and founder of Reiki Rays Institute www.reikiraysinstitute.com, and is currently the Executive Director of the World Metaphysical Association www.worldmeta.org.

Made in United States
Troutdale, OR
09/14/2023